THE CELL BLOCK PRESENTS...

GET OUT, STAY OUT

Mike Enemigo & Shane Bowen

Published by: THE CELL BLOCK™

THE CELL BLOCK
P.O. Box 1025
Rancho Cordova, CA 95741

Facebook.com/thecellblock.net

Copyright© 2019 By Shane Bowen

Cover design by Mike Enemigo
Edited by Ricky Decidido

Send comments, reviews, or other business inquiries:
thecellblock.net@mail.com
Visit our website: thecellblock.net

A Letter From The Cell Block:

You have in your hands a book that continues the interesting tradition of The Cell Block. That word "tradition" is a proud one: How could I know back in January of 2014 that my venture as author and publisher would be so successful? Yet, we have followed very well my original plan to publish books principally for prisoners, and always   by prisoners, that now, from a start with five books in January of 2014 we've reached twenty, and counting. It is fair to say that we have a tradition of publishing such books.

This book teaches basic and advanced topics related to preparing to go before a parole board and to get out of prison by being truly ready for the parole hearing and reentry to society. It teaches about honest self-change that will accomplish what was somehow lacking before going to prison – you will be positive, caring, honest, and correct in "the way you think, the things you say, and the way you conduct yourself" (Chapter 17).

But the book doesn't stop with your exit from prison; it goes on to teach about the tough and important work needed to Stay Out! – continuing the change process, continuing to use your support network, continuing your progress until you are unassailable. This book does not replace any programs the prisons offer that help you change your life, nor replace nor speed up nor make easier the hard work you must do. The book, in fact, urges you to participate in all the available programs, and teaches how to get more benefit by attending with the committed purpose of self-improvement. It inspires to avoid the attitude of fellow inmates who attend only to get credit or a certificate, but who then hypocritically resume (or they've never stopped) the actions and behaviors their attendance and participation were supposed to stop, if only they'd paid attention.

Yes, this book inspires that, and more; it is rich in information, procedures, ideas, tips, and resources, but overall its thrust is clearly to inspire you to enter and stay on a path of self-improvement that will lead to release from prison and afterwards to success in society, with no further criminal activity.

The Cell Block is too proud to provide such a complete and important guide. We commend it to you, and offer every good wish for your success in achieving the goals urged in the book. We welcome your comments, whether critical or praising, whether pointing out what might be missing or incomplete, or telling us how some part of the book helped you change forever.

Sincerely,

Mike

YOUR RESPONSIBILITY WHEN USING THIS GUIDE

When putting together *GET OUT! STAY OUT!* The Secrets to Getting Out of Prison and Staying Out for Good, we did our best to provide useful and accurate information that you can use to:

1. Increase your odds of obtaining a release date through the board process;

2. Better yourself and your future by learning and understanding the information, tips, and concepts provided; and

3. Increase your odds of staying out of prison once and for all! Please remember, this guide provides only general information. We do not provide legal advice, and the content does not represent the official policy of the administration of any jail, prison, probation or parole authority, or of any other agency or individual.

TABLE OF CONTENTS

GET OUT, STAY OUT!
PART ONE:

GET OUT! PREPARING FOR BOARD HEARINGS

The information in Part One is intended for you who need to prepare for Board hearings. There are many areas that the Board will evaluate to determine if you are suitable for parole, or not. By giving you an in-depth look into the whole process, you can cover all bases and greatly increase your odds of being found suitable.

CHAPTER 1

The Board and Parole Suitability

The parole process for you, the Lifer with a term-to-life sentence, involves an interaction between you, who would like to get out and stay out, and the Board, the official agency that interviews you and decides on your suitability. The Board will review your entire record before the hearing; your current qualifications may show in the record, but your actual qualifications WILL be revealed by your answers and demeanor when you face the Board at the hearing. This chapter opens Part One – about the Board, the hearing, and how to prepare – and describes the Board and "suitability" for parole; it is the first of several chapters of information that will prove useful to you, the Lifer, and your attorney, as you seek to obtain a parole date from the Board.

The Board

The Board is the agency responsible for determining whether and when Lifers can be released on parole. For prisoners sentenced to life with the possibility of parole, the Board is authorized to determine whether and when those Lifers are released from prison. The only standard in the law to be granted parole is that the prisoner show he is not a current

1

danger to society; however, the path to that finding is left largely to the "discretion" of the Board's Commissioners.

The Commissioners look to a core list of items they feel show suitability or lack thereof:

1. The life crime. Although the Board, by court decision, can no longer use the crime alone as a reason for denial, nearly all Decisions issued by the Board mention the "heinous" or "cold" or "cruel" nature of the crime.

2. Lack of "remorse" or "insight" into how the prisoner came to commit the crime. This finding is often based on the psychological evaluation given to all Lifers shortly before their hearings.

3. Lack of sufficient self-help or rehabilitative programming.

4. Insufficient or incomplete parole plans.

These are the main reasons used by the Board to show that prisoners still pose an unreasonable danger to society and thus justify denial of parole. The courts have held that the smallest provable deficiency in any of these areas is enough for the Board to find a prisoner unsuitable. Each area must be addressed and dealt with, so in the following chapters we will go deeper into detail about addressing these core areas, as well as others. Our goal is to help you and your attorney be as prepared as possible in your presentation that will prove to the board that you are, in fact, suitable for parole.

Parole Consideration

When the Board first meets with a Lifer, they will review the prisoner's file, document the prisoner's conduct and activities during his or her incarceration, and make recommendations regarding prison programs. This first meeting is sometimes called a "documentation hearing," and is held in the year before the Lifer is eligible for parole. Subsequent Lifer hearings offer a chance at parole, and are called "parole consideration hearings."

The main issue before the Board at a Lifer hearing is whether the prisoner should be found suitable for parole. If the Board panel that conducts the parole consideration hearing decides that the prisoner is not suitable for parole, then the panel will also determine how many years the prisoner must wait before being reconsidered for parole at a subsequent hearing. In most cases, prisoners are denied parole repeatedly over the course of many years and many consideration hearings.

The Board takes into consideration such factors as the nature of the prisoner's offense, the felony conviction record, the probability of reformation, and the interests of public safety. Any release date earlier than the maximum sentence (usually, life) is supposed to reflect a recognition of the prisoner's efforts at rehabilitation.

Parole Suitability

Let's discuss some factors that are used to determine parole suitability. The decision regarding parole suitability must take into account all relevant and reliable information. The Board has also established specific regulations to guide its parole decision in determining whether a prisoner is likely to pose a danger to society if released from prison. A prisoner will be found unsuitable if the Board finds the prisoner would pose an unreasonable risk of danger to society if released from prison.

Factors tending to show suitability for parole include the lack of a juvenile record, a history of stable relationships with others, signs of remorse and taking responsibility for the crime, motivation for the crime (very stressful or traumatic conditions leading up to, or at the time of, the offense), lack of a criminal history, age at time of offense, plans for the future, and institutional behavior.

Other information the panel may consider includes the prisoner's social history, past and present mental state, behavior before, during, and after the crime for which the prisoner was sentenced, past and present attitude toward the crime, any conditions of treatment or control, and current community contacts outside the institution, and the support of such people.

Parole Suitability Rights

Generally, Lifers are entitled to basic procedural rights concerning their parole suitability hearings: Notice of the scheduled hearing at least 60 days in advance; assistance of an attorney, at state's expense if necessary; an opportunity to review all non-confidential information which the Board uses in reaching its decision; an unbiased hearing panel; an opportunity to present documents for the panel's consideration; assistance in preparing for and participating in the hearing, including accommodations for any disability as defined in the Americans with Disabilities Act (ADA). A Lifer also has a right to personal appearance and participation at the hearing, and to have an opportunity to postpone, waive, or continue the hearing, or to stipulate to being unsuitable. After the hearing, the Lifer must timely receive a verbatim transcript of the hearing and a written statement of the panel's Decision.

Attorney for Hearing

A Lifer's attorney should review the prisoner's Central File, including the sentencing transcript, work and education reports, and chronos; the attorney should develop a well-documented statement of the Lifer's in-prison conduct. If there are disciplinary write-ups, any mitigating circumstances surrounding the occurrences may be presented to the panel. The Board looks very unfavorably upon disciplinary write-ups, and the Lifer's attorney should minimize them and emphasize all positive aspects of the prisoner's in-prison conduct. More on "Your Attorney's Role" in Chapter 5.

Consecutive Terms

Some life prisoners may also receive sentences to be served consecutively to the life term. Generally, a prisoner who receives a life term and who also receives a consecutive term serves the consecutive term first. The time served on the consecutive term does not count towards the life term. However, if a consecutive term is received for crimes committed in prison while already serving a life term, the consecutive term does not interrupt the life term, but is to be served after the life term is completed.

Life Without the Possibility of Parole (LWOP)

In some cases, a criminal defendant may receive a sentence of Life Without the Possibility of Parole (LWOP). Persons convicted of First Degree Murder with Special Circumstances must receive either the death penalty or an LWOP sentence. Some other crimes may also be punished by such a sentence. LWOP prisoners are not considered for release on parole in the same way as prisoners sentenced to terms of life with the possibility of parole, usually a term-to-life sentence, e.g., 15-to-life. The procedures for Lifer parole hearings do not apply to LWOP prisoners.

Federal Court Cases Related to Parole Consideration

In contrast to the very slim chances that a Lifer will be granted parole through the normal parole consideration process, some Lifers have found success in the courts. Prior to the year 2000, almost no courts were willing to grant prisoners relief in their challenges to the denial of their parole. Since that time, however, many cases have been decided that impact the parole consideration process – some negatively, but some very positively.

The Ninth Circuit Court of Appeal has indicated that Due Process may prohibit parole officials from repeatedly relying on the Commitment offense and other long-past misbehavior to deny parole, stating that "[a] continued reliance in the future on an unchanging factor, the circumstance of the offense and conduct prior to imprisonment, runs contrary to the rehabilitative goals espoused by the prison system and could result in a Due Process violation." Biggs v. Terhune (2003) 334 F.3d 910, 917. Since then, the Ninth Circuit Court of Appeal has overturned a parole reversal that improperly relied on the life prisoner's long-past criminal offense, which no longer provided reliable evidence of current dangerousness in light of the prisoner's history of rehabilitation. Hayward v. Marshall (9th Cir. 2008) 512 F.3d 536. Lower federal courts (the District courts) have reached similar conclusions. Rosenkrantz v. Marshal (C.D. Cal. 2006) 444 F.Supp.2d 1063, 1081, 1084 (holding that "after nearly twenty years of rehabilitation, the ability to predict a prisoner's future dangerousness based simply on the circumstances of his or her crime is nil."); Martin v. Marshal (N.D. Cal. 2006) 431 F.Supp.2d 1038, 1047-1048.

Three Goals a Lifer Should Have at a Board Hearing

The first goal is to persuade the Board to grant parole by demonstrating that the "suitability" factors in the Board's regulations apply, and that the "unsuitability" factors do not.

The second goal, if not granted parole, should be to obtain the shortest possible period of parole denial and/or limit the number of issues the Board will be concerned about in the future.

The third goal is to establish a strong record that will increase the chances of success if the life prisoner decides to bring a court challenge after parole is denied.

CHAPTER 2

Understanding the Parole Process

Before you can prepare for a parole hearing, you need to understand how the process works. The next few chapters will give you some valuable information, but the laws and regulations about parole are complicated, so not everything can be explained here. The goal is to give you as much information and as many resources as possible, so that you can be as prepared as possible. Also, please understand that this is not legal advice; it is information. The State will appoint an attorney to represent you at your hearing, or you can hire a private attorney. That attorney must explain the process to you and answer your questions about the laws and regulations. Your attorney will also review your case and give you specific advice on how to prepare for your hearing. (Chapter 5 further discusses the role of your attorney.)

How Does the Board Decide Whether or Not to Grant Parole?

The law requires the Board to grant parole unless it finds "some evidence" that you would pose a danger to the community if released. The most common reasons that Commissioners use to deny parole are:

- Recent and/or violent disciplinary violations;
- Recent gang involvement;
- Recent substance abuse;
- Lack of credibility or lack of truthfulness;
- Lack of remorse for your actions;
- Lack of insight (failing to understand why the crime happened and its effect on others);
- Lack of realistic parole plans or lack of proof (documentation) supporting those plans; and
- Information contained in your Confidential File.

What Are the Three Key Questions the Board Wants Answered?

The Board is essentially looking for truthful answers to the following big questions:

1) Do you take full responsibility for your crime?
- Do you fully admit to your offense without excuses?
- Can you be truthful about all of your intentions and choices before, during, and after the crime?
- Have you thought deeply about how your choices impacted others?
- Do you understand the effect your crime had on others (the victim, the victim's family and friends, the community, your family, and others)?
- If the Board determines your testimony at the hearing is not credible, you will probably be denied parole.

2) Have you explored and do you understand why you committed the crime(s), i.e., the "causative factors":
- Have you thought deeply about the things that led you to commit the crime?

- What kind of person were you at the time of the crime?
- What kind of lifestyle were you living?
- Can you describe the choices you make, the perspectives you had, the situations you put yourself in that made it possible for you to commit the crime?

Have you faced the challenges and traumas in your life that may have influenced your choices and character?

The Board is looking for explanations, but not excuses, for any negatives: the crime(s), your prior lies about the crime, your prior lifestyle, or your negative behavior in prison.

3) What have you done to address the things in your life that led to you committing the crime? Have you sincerely faced the issues in your life that led to criminal behavior?
How are you different today? How does the way you live your life now show that you have addressed and overcome the causative factors of the crime? Does your disciplinary history reflect who you are today? How do you make choices today?

What values guide your choices?

What are some specific lessons or life skills that you have learned from programs that you've done in prison? How have you grown and matured? What are your biggest strengths and weaknesses? What is your character?
The Board expects that you have matured and benefitted from your period of incarceration. Part of maturity is understanding your own strengths and weaknesses. Your answers to this third set of questions extremely important, as they are the forward-looking issues.
You need to have real answers to these questions for the Board. You cannot fake it at a parole hearing. Preparing to

answer these questions is hard work and can lead you to spend time thinking about very sensitive or difficult issues in your life that you may have ignored up to now, because facing them squarely is uncomfortable, painful, or hard. But the truth is, you can only get to the real answers for these questions if you spend the time and do the hard work that is necessary to think these things through. These questions require you to reach down to the very core of what shaped your choices and how you lived your life at the time of the crime. As you read this right now, you might be thinking these ideas sound "touchy-feely," or not related to who you are now; however, addressing these issues will increase your ability to show the Board how much you have learned, matured, and changed while incarcerated.

One of the best ways to get started is to discuss the questions with another person. Choose someone you trust and who will give you honest feedback and support as you work through things. Beware of revealing incriminating information that could be used against you later. If you do not have a "safe" person or place to discuss these topics, you can instead write about them. Once you start working with an attorney, it will be important to discuss these issues with him or her. Information on these topics will be discussed throughout this book.

What Happens at the Parole Hearing

This section provides an overview of the basics of the proceedings at a parole hearing, so you know what to expect as you prepare. It is just a starting point. Who will be at the hearing?

• You: you will answer questions under oath throughout the bulk of the hearing. After your attorney's closing statement, you have the right to make your own brief (about five minutes) closing statement, if you wish.

• Your attorney: you can hire your own attorney, or the Board will appoint one to your case. It is the Board's expectation that an appointed attorney will meet with you no later than 45 days prior to the hearing. Your attorney will have a chance to ask you questions during the hearing so you can clarify any issues that might be unclear for the Commissioners. Your attorney can also make objections and give a closing statement.

• Commissioners: One Commissioner (sometimes two) and one Deputy Commissioner from the Board of Parole Hearings will run the hearing. They will have reviewed all of the records in your case, and they will review any paperwork you present at the hearing. They will ask most of the questions during the hearing, and they will make the decision to grant or deny parole to you.

• District Attorney: A District Attorney from the County of Commitment may attend the hearing (in person, by video, or by phone). He or she will have an opportunity to ask questions, and to make a closing statement. He or she may say things that are untrue.

• Victims: The victim(s) and/or the families of victim(s) may be present (in person, by video, or by phone). They are allowed to make a statement at the end of the hearing. If they are not present, or by their choice, a victim's representative may read letters from victims or victim's families.

• Others: There will also be a correctional officer in the room, and there may be a few neutral observers. None of these people speak at the hearing.

What will happen during the hearing?

Everyone else will be seated before you and your attorney come into the hearing room. There will be some fidgeting while the panel makes sure the recording equipment is working, and the meeting will be officially convened: the

Commissioner will announce your name and number for the benefit of the recorded transcript, and will give the date and time of the hearing. The panel will say hello to you; this is not a false courtesy – no matter how tough their questioning may later become, they are trained to attempt a neutral approach, and will try to maintain this posture throughout, unless you start disrespecting them or the process by being snide, evasive, or untruthful. They will also be watching your body language, so be courteous, controlled, and careful.

You will be sworn in, promising to tell the truth. Everyone in the room will be introduced (with names spelled out, so the transcriber can later identify voices in the recording, and get the transcript mostly right). Remember to speak clearly, you want EVERYTHING you say to be understandable on that very important recording.

Usually the order of subjects is logical. First, they will ask you some things about yourself. Then, the hearing will discuss pre-conviction factors: your entire life up to and including the life crime. Next, the hearing will examine post-conviction factors: your life in prison, including the good and (especially) the bad. The next subject will be your parole plans and the support you expect from your family and friends, whether you're headed to a reentry program, where you plan to live, what you plan to do. Finally, at the end (or maybe distributed throughout), the panel will discuss your attitudes, your rehabilitation, the psychologist's report, and any challenges they may have if they think some of your answers are not right. This is all discussed at greater length elsewhere in this book (see Chapter 4).

How does the hearing end (closing statements and the Decision)?

The District Attorney, followed by your attorney and you, and the victim (or the victim's next-of-kin or representative) will be allowed to make closing statements. In addition to affirming points in favor of suitability, your attorney should focus on the key parts of what was discussed at the hearing. Your attorney should also respond directly to the District Attorney's statement (the D.A. will likely have spoken extremely negatively, at least). Your attorney may want to conclude the closing statement with a plea that reminds the panel of the most appealing parts of your case.

The panel will also ask you if you want to make a closing statement, or whether you want to rest on whatever you attorney said. Some prisoners choose to read a written statement, which is acceptable; in fact, it may be the best approach if you have difficulty expressing yourself verbally under stressful circumstances. You will want to use the opportunity to express remorse for the crime and victims, to explain how you have changed in the years since the crime was committed, and to convince the panel that you are motivated and capable of succeeding on parole.

Lastly, the victim, next-of-kin, or representative will be given an opportunity to address the panel.

And the Decision?

After closing statements, the panel will take a recess and send everyone out of the room. Their deliberations can take anywhere from a few minutes to more than an hour. When they call the parties back in, they will read their Decision. If any part of the Decision is unclear, or could be challenged, your attorney should question the panel closely to get your objections and get the panel's answers on the record.

The panel must also issue it's Decision in writing and state the reasons for its Decision, and identify the statements, recommendations, and materials it relied on in reaching its Decision. The Decision will be to either grant or deny parole, or there may be a tie vote between the two panel members.

If the Decision is "Parole Denied"?

By far the most common decision following a parole hearing is to find the prisoner unsuitable for parole. As part of the Decision, the panel will also state when you may next be considered for parole suitability. If parole is denied, your next hearing may be scheduled in three years, five years, or, if you were convicted of murder, in up to fifteen years. With a denial, the panel will typically also give advice as to areas of rehabilitation for your focus in the ensuing years, as, get your GED, have no rules violations, etc.

If the panel gives a "Split Decision"?

If one panel member believes that you are suitable for parole, and the other panel member votes to deny parole, there is a split decision. There will also be a split decision if the panel members cannot agree on the appropriate length of the parole denial period. In either situation, the case will be sent for a review by the entire Board.

If the Decision is "Parole Granted"?

If parole is granted, it means that the Board found the Lifer to be suitable for release. The Board then turns its attention to determining how much time the prisoner should serve in prison before actually being released. Usually, by the time the Board grants parole, the prisoner will have served long past the applicable minimum term, and so his or her proper release date will already have been long past.

You and your attorney should be aware that the Decision granting parole is not final, and release will not occur, until after the panel's Decision has been reviewed by the entire Board, and, in some cases, by the Governor.

15

What You and Your Family Should Remember

The parole process is complex, heavily discretionary, and very often frustrating to both you and your family. Families want to be supportive and helpful, but often can't understand why their loved one isn't coming home, despite exemplary institutional behavior, letters of support, and years – even decades – in prison.

There are no exact answers to how to be found suitable, but there are some actions both you and your family can take to make the chances of receiving a date from the Board more favorable. The two most important points for you and your family are these:

1) Don't give up hope. Parole is possible, and in more and more cases it is happening.
2) Be realistic about the time and work needed to successfully gain a date. You can't just simply do your time and stay discipline-free-the Board wants to see real rehabilitation. There is work involved, and it's up to you to get it done.

There are a lot of things you must do within the institutional setting to get that actual rehabilitation, and proof of that rehabilitation, that will tilt that "possibility" more in your favor. Of course, you'll need to avoid disciplinary write-ups (or anything in your record that's negative, like too-frequent bed moves or job changes); but you'll also need plenty of positives, like education and a GED or college classes; like job preparation with vocational classes; like satisfactory and long-term participation in self-help groups either specific to your own situation (perhaps Criminal Gang member Anonymous, or Alcoholics Anonymous), or generally recognized as important and useful: Anger Management, Technology classes, and so on. Lastly, though there's less opportunity, volunteerism is helpful; participate in the Cancer Walks and charity fund-raisers; become a mentor or trainer in one of the groups; be active in your Church. Any and all of these things provide both real rehabilitation and proof of that rehabilitation, and improve your chances of parole.

CHAPTER 3

The Information Used in the Parole Process

The Board has access to all of the records concerning you, which include documents not only from your current sentence and your in-prison doings, but other documents as well, for example the primary documents in your criminal case, where the Probation Officer's Report, at least, can be expected to be somewhat prejudicial. There may be documents from any previous investigation, including who-knows-what about your past, good or bad. The Board may see any of this, and in this age of instant availability, the panel might have it all at the table in a little desktop. A portion of the record is assembled by the "inmate records" department, and is provided to the Board and to your attorney; this is called the "parole packet." If you haven't looked at your record, you really ought to, and take steps under law to correct or counter whatever's not right. The only part of your Central File that you won't be permitted to see is the confidential section (and they won't let your attorney see it either, but he should look at everything else; it's not all in the parole packet).

Reading this chapter will clue you in as to just how important are your records, and why you should keep a watch on them.

What Information Will the Board Be Reviewing?

The Board will read and consider everything in your Central File (C-File). This may include, but is not limited to:

Case paperwork (witness interviews, police reports, trial transcripts, probation reports, autopsy results, Appellate decision).
- All disciplinary write-ups and grievances.
- Psychological evaluations (see below).
- Transcripts of prior parole hearings.
- Certificates and vocations.

Positive and negative chronos for programs or from staff. Victim statements.
- Confidential information.
- Board Report (prepared by your Correctional Counselor; includes an "Inmate Version of Events" that needs to be accurate and truthful).
- The Board will also read and consider any documents you and your attorney submit to the Commissioners. These may include:

Documentation of parole plans.
- Letters of support from you family and people in the community who know you.
- Insight Statement (not required, but might help). This is something you write that includes a description of your understanding of the harm you have caused and your feelings about that harm.
- Self-help and book reports on self-help or other books (necessary when formal programs in prisons are limited). Relapse prevention plan.

Psychological Evaluations (Comprehensive Risk Assessments)

19

Before you appear at a hearing for parole consideration, the Board will secure a psychological evaluation, called a "Comprehensive Risk Assessment", to predict whether you present a low, medium, or high risk of future violence. The assessment will also contain other information – about whether you accept responsibility for your actions, whether you understand why your crime happened, and whether you have participated in the right kind and number of programs to address the factors that contributed to your crime. If your hearing is a California Youth Offender Hearing, the assessment prepared must also take into consideration the diminished culpability of youth as compared to adults, the hallmark features of youth, and any subsequent growth and increased maturity you have undergone as an individual. The Board's psychologists address this requirement by adding a section to their assessments that directly discusses those youth factors.

Your evaluation will include a meeting and interview with a Board psychologist, which will usually take place at least a couple of months before the scheduled parole hearing. This meeting is very important, and you should approach it as you would your Board hearing. The psychologist will be evaluating and considering the same factors that the Board considers, and the Board will rely on the conclusions of the psychologist. You will receive a written copy of the psychologist's assessment well before your hearing. Plan to discuss the assessment with your attorney, and be sure to identify for the attorney anything in it that you think is inaccurate.

If you have done positive things like reading books, doing correspondence classes, making plans for parole, creating a relapse prevention plan, or getting support letters from your family, try to get documentation of these before your psychological evaluation. You can ask your counselor to put copies of this kind of documentation in your C-File before the evaluation; however, you should also make sure to bring your own copies of this documentation with you when you go to the evaluation, so the psychologist who is evaluating you can see all the good things you are doing before he or she writes the assessment.

What Are Some Concerns With Risk Assessment?

Antisocial Personality Disorder ("ASPD") is commonly asserted by the Board's psychologists. The diagnosis of ASPD is important because the Board weighs it as a big risk factor for future criminality. Besides the negative effect on parole consideration, diagnosis of ASPD carries a serious stigma for an individual in the community.

The DSM-5 definition of ASPD centers on behavior that shows "a pervasive pattern of disregard for and violation of the rights of others." The diagnosis requires three or more of the following behaviors or traits:

1) Failure to conform to or respect laws or social norms, as indicated by repeatedly performing acts that are grounds for arrest.

2) Deceitfulness, as indicated by repeated lying, use of aliases, or conning (deceiving) others for personal profit or pleasure.

3) Impulsivity or failure to plan ahead, as indicated by decisions made on the spur of the moment without forethought or consideration of the consequences, sudden changes jobs, residence, or relationships.

4) Irritability and aggressiveness, as indicated by repeated physical fights or assaults. It doesn't include aggressive acts to defend oneself or others.

5) Reckless disregard for the safety of self or others. It may be seen in recurrent speeding, DUIs, or accidents; risky

sexual behavior or substance abuse, disregard or neglect of children, and so forth.

6) Consistent irresponsibility, as indicated by repeated failure to maintain good work behavior or honor financial obligations. It can be seen in long periods of unemployment, frequent quitting of jobs, absences from work, or defaulting on debts, child support, and other support obligations.

7) Lack of remorse, as indicated by being indifferent to or rationalizing having hurt, mistreated, or stolen from another. The person may offer a superficial rationalization for such behavior, somehow minimize the harm that was done, or blame the victims.

The psychologist should avoid making such a diagnosis when the qualifying factors are very old, or markedly disjoint in time, and have been replaced, through rehabilitative efforts, with appropriate personal behaviors.

Letters of Support

Letters of support from friends and family are a vitally important part of the documents that a prisoner presents to the Board for parole consideration. However, these need to be carefully crafted, meet certain requirements, and be sent to specific locations. Your family and friends who write such letters should try to keep them to one page and specific as to what support they can offer and for how long they are prepared to offer that support, bullet point for clarity. Their letters should describe their relationship with you, how you have grown as a person, and what impact they have had on your life.

Letters should be sent approximately six months prior to the parole hearing. Letters must be updated for each parole hearing; they must be original documents and signed. If not signed, they will not be considered valid.

Send all letters, as well as confirmation of other support, such as job offers, to the "Lifer Desk" at the prison housing the Lifer, with copies to the prisoner, to the attorney, and to the prisoner's counselor at the prison.

What is insight?

One of the most important areas you must focus on in preparing for a parole hearing is your insight into the violent tendencies and the risk factors that trigger them. You should do everything possible to show understanding of past criminal or violent actions, the causes of the behavior, how to avoid these causes, and why they are no longer an issue. Any therapeutic programming, such as Anger Management or Cognitive Therapy programs, should be pointed out. Similarly, if alcohol or drug abuse was a causative factor, you should do everything possible to show understanding of how and why you got involved with the substance abuse; you should demonstrate that you've overcome addiction and built defenses against the triggers; you should already have a relapse prevention effort in place that's working in prison and that will extend into life outside as part of your parole plans, which must include both support from concerned persons and attendance at AA or NA, or some equivalent program.

If you've internalized the antidotes to anger and violence, if you've conquered substance abuse, if you are clear of any write-ups for these issues for a long time (as you must work VERY hard to be) even though anger and violence are common in prison and alcohol and drugs are readily available, you should point out your efforts and achievements to the psychological evaluator, and ask him or her to provide a severity rating and include the "in remission" specifier. Remember, the Board will want you to discuss, both verbally and in writing, specifically how you will remain violence-free and sober once released from prison.

What Is a Good Insight Statement?

One way to help the Board see that you have insight is by preparing an Insight Statement; however, the written statement is meaningless if your testimony during the hearing does not show that you have a deep understanding of the factors contributing to your crime and that you have taken specific steps to address those factors. A good Insight Statement should include:

1) A complete account of the commitment offense from beginning to end;

2) A discussion of causative factors: how you got to the point of committing your crime;

3) How you have changed and addressed your causative factors; and

4) Your remorse for committing the crime.

Remorse and Responsibility

The Board's latest buzzword has two parts: Contributing Factors and Responsibility. If substance abuse or anger issues figured in the life crime, you must admit to the contributing factors but stress it was not drugs, alcohol, or anger that caused the crime: it was your decision to indulge in those behaviors. Whatever the contributing factors, the ultimate responsibility for the crime lies with you and must be accepted by you.

Expressions of remorse or amends must be genuine. These need to be in your own words, not stock phrases and words memorized from self-help books and programs. Letters of remorse should be written to the victim(s) and/or families, whether they are ever received or not. Keep copies. Write out your statement for the Board, and don't be afraid to read it at the hearing. You lose no points for reading rather than

24

memorizing the statement, and reading it will insure you cover all the issues you want to in the way that you want to.

Self-Help and Book Reports

The Board will look at your recent achievements, present state of mind, and likelihood of successful reintegration into society. The best way to show the Board these things is with certificates of completion from self-help groups and with book reports. These are the several areas of self-help you should focus on:

1) AA and NA programs are helpful not only for substance abuse issues, but can be used by all prisoners to show serious dedication to rehabilitation.

2) Go beyond the GED; Take College or correspondence courses, if possible; use self-study books on subjects that interest you and that will help on parole: books on how to write résumés, on social skills, on parenting, on relationship building, etc.

3) Write book reports on books you read. These should be meaningful reports showing how the steps or lessons in the books relate to your situation, and how you will use and apply them in your life. Reports of books about victims' experiences and recovery can be used to understand and exhibit empathy.

4) If causative factors were present in the life crime (addictions, anger), the Board will want to see how you have learned to deal with them.

5) Repair fractured relationships. Part of making amends and gaining insight is to reach out to family and friends who may have been hurt by your past behaviors and to initiate repair of those relationships. Be sure to address how the crime impacted others in your family and the community at large.

6) Consider securing a private psychological examination.

What Is a Good Relapse Prevention Plan?

A relapse prevention plan should explain how you will avoid returning to drugs, alcohol, gangs, criminality, etc. (depending on the specifics of your life and crime), and should include:

1) Warning signs for relapse in your life (sometimes called triggers or stressors);

2) An explanation of how you will deal with those triggers and stressors so that you do not relapse; and

3) a list of tools and resources you can use on the outside to prevent relapse.

Behavior Change

When it comes to behavior change, it's up to you to fill in the blanks for the Board. Without trying to comment on criticisms or debates about these tools, you should make sure the materials you submit to the Board emphasize the changes and improvements you have achieved since you came to prison, how you accomplished those changes, and how long it's been since the negative acts that led to the crime and a prison term. You should list accomplishments and activities that demonstrate your suitability and your compliance with rules and expectations.

It is also important to address the impact of age, and the steps you took to reinforce the natural tendency for substance abuse, crime, and violence to subside with age. It is also important for supporters, in their letters, to show how you have changed over time to become much more "pro-social," responsible, loving, empathic, motivated to succeed, etc., and to explain why they are convinced you are not a risk for future substance abuse, crime, or violence.

CHAPTER 4

What Will Be Discussed at the Hearing?

Most of the hearing will be devoted to discussion of the various case facts that may reflect upon your suitability for parole. Generally, much of the hearing will be taken up by the panel members reciting the case facts and asking you specific questions. Most of the panel's recitations of fact, and their questions, will be based on information found in the Board Packet and elsewhere in the Central File, which will usually be sitting open in front of the Deputy Commissioner. Most of their comments will be based on information received since the last parole hearing. You will be given an opportunity to add anything the panel fails to mention; therefore, if older accomplishments are not mentioned (such as educational or vocational certificates), you should be prepared to inform the panel of those accomplishments.

Commitment Offense

The Board will ask many questions about your commitment offense. Generally, the Board will read facts into the record (from the Appellate decision or the Probation Report), and then ask if you agree with those facts. If you do not agree, the Board will allow you to state your own version. It is important to remember the Board will not decide all over again whether you were guilty of your crime. However, it may be important to correct any inaccurate facts about the crime. What facts, if any, you should correct is something that you should decide with your attorney's help. The most important thing is that the Board expects you to be truthful about the crime and your role in it. And, the Board will be listening to how you describe the crime and whether you appear to be making excuses for your behavior or downplaying (minimizing) the effect of your crime. The Board wants to see if you have insight into your commitment offense and remorse for the impact of your actions, and that you do not deflect responsibility.

If you've had a prior parole hearing, the panel will announce that they are adopting the statement of facts from the previous hearing, from the Probation Officer's Report, or from a Court of Appeal decision if you appealed your conviction. If there was a trial, the panel will assume the truth of the facts found by a judge or jury. If there was no trial, your attorney should make sure that the record clearly shows that there was no factual finding by any court regarding the underlying facts. In such instances, you and your attorney may want to introduce additional information about the crime through witnesses (if possible) or documents relaying statements of the trial counsel, prosecutor, trial judge, crime partners, or family members.

Because the facts of the crime are weighed heavily by the hearing panel, it is important to prevent the panel from basing its Decision on misrepresentations about the crime. Your attorney should be prepared to rebut misleading or unsupported allegations made in the Probation Report of by the District Attorney, and should suggest an alternative source for the statement of facts.

There may be some facts related to the crime that tend to show suitability. These include facts showing that you committed the crime as a result of significant stress in your life, especially if the stress had built over a long period of time. Another fact that may show suitability for parole is that you have shown remorse, such as by attempting to repair the damage, seeking help for or relieving suffering of the victim, or giving indications that you understand the nature and magnitude of the offense.

Criminal and Social History

The Board will also discuss your life before your crime. This is often called "Social History." The Board can ask questions about anything in your life prior to the commitment offense. They are likely to ask about your family life and upbringing, your neighborhood, your school, and your friends and relationships. The Board wants to know about positive activities (like sports, jobs, school, hobbies) and things that may have hurt you in some way (like learning difficulties, physical or sexual abuse, neglect, exposure to violence in your home or neighborhood, gang involvement, drug and alcohol use, criminal history). The Board wants to understand the person you were and the things that may have led to your crime (causative factors).

As with the offense, the Board is likely to rely heavily on the Probation Report. Some of the information may also come from information provided by you during the psychological evaluation. You and your attorney should try to correct or rebut inaccurate or particularly damaging statements about your prior history. If at all possible, these efforts would be supported by documents or witness statements.

The Board regulations mention specific factors related to criminal and social history that tend to show unsuitability or suitability. The list of possible unsuitability factors includes, for example, that you have a previous record of violence, a history of unstable or tumultuous relationships with others, or a history of committing sadistic sexual offenses. The acknowledged suitability factors include, for example, that you have no juvenile record of assaulting others, or committing crimes with a potential of personal harm to victims, have a history of reasonably stable relationships with others, or lack any significant history of violent crime.

Post-Commitment Factors

The Board will also discuss what you have done since you were incarcerated. This is an important part of the hearing that allows you to show how you have changed. This is your chance to demonstrate your growth, maturity, and positive changes, and to prove rehabilitation. The Board will discuss your 1) disciplinary history; 2) education, jobs, and programming; 3) any positive chronos; and 4) your psychological evaluations. If you have a history of gang involvement in prison, the Board will most likely ask you about that as well. The Board wants to see evidence that you are on a different path than you were at the time of the crime.

Your programming in prison will be a major topic of discussion at the hearing. Your attorney should show how you have taken advantage of every opportunity to be involved in education, job, charitable, and self-help programs. If you have good in-prison behavior, you should emphasize that fact, especially if you were fairly young when the offense was committed and you appear to have become more mature over time. If you perform well in a job, a vocation, or in education, and participate in self-help groups and programs, you will also be a better candidate for parole.

On the other hand, disciplinary violations are likely to be cited as factors supporting denial of parole. Also, counseling chronos, poor work or school performance, or refusal to participate in self-help programs will likely be viewed

30

unfavorably by the Board. You and your attorney should do your best to try to explain why such behavior problems do not show that you are currently dangerous. For example, your attorney will want to point out that your disciplinary violations are all or mostly from years past, or are entirely non-violent; you may also want to explain how and why you have made a turn-around since the time of the disciplinary offenses.

Your attorney should also be alert to any programming recommendations the Board makes that are impossible for you to fulfill. For example, the Board should not rely on failure to participate in programs that are not available to you, perhaps due to a disability. Also remember that if you claim to have participated in AA or NA, the Board might ask you to recite and discuss some of the 12 steps.

Parole Plans

Finally, you must have realistic parole plans and provide documentation of those plans. Documentation is proof, and usually it is in the form of letters from the people offering you support when you get out. It is important to have very specific parole plans. In addition, you should have at least one back-up option in case your first choice does not work. The Board tends to look favorably on plans that include a period of time in a recognized live-in reentry program.

The Panel will discuss your parole plans in an attempt to determine whether you have made realistic plans for release or have developed marketable skills that can be put to use upon release. The panel will ask specific questions about where you will live and work, and raise any concerns related to alcohol or substance abuse treatment while on parole. The panel will also review your support letters to confirm offers of residence, employment, and treatment. You should be prepared to answer tough questions, such as "How do we know you won't commit another crime?"

The 10 Key Things You Should Present

You should do as much thinking and planning for release as you can before you meet with the Board, and make sure the Board knows the plans you have in place. Here are the 10 key things you should have ready to present to the parole panel at the hearing; be sure to address each of these 10 aspects:

1) Employment: Although a confirmed job is not a legal requirement to be found suitable for parole, and may in fact not be attainable for some Lifers, you should show diligence in seeking employment. A) Prepare a résumé. B) Show research into likely jobs in your parole area. C) Letters of intent from prospective employers are very useful, even offers of employment in your family's business. D) The Board is interested in seeing you have a plan for providing yourself with the funds needed for living.

2) Relapse Prevention Plan: Have one ready and written, and A) Know where and when support groups meet in your parole area, and who to contact for help with emergency finances, housing, and counseling. B) It is good to already have an AA or NA sponsor before release, to carry over from prison into outside life.

3) Short Term and Long Term Plans: Good plans can improve your chances. A) Show the Board you realize that reintegration is a process, not just getting out of prison. B) Short-term plans can include obtaining identity cards, Social Security cards, and enrolling in school.

4) Stable Relationship(s): Don't get married just to help your parole plans, but if that event is in your plans anyway, a spouse can provide evidence of a stable relationship and support on the outside. (See items 6 & 7, also.)

5) Professional Services: Substance abuse counseling or prevention services, medical or pharmaceutical services for conditions like ADHD or bipolar disorder, plans for ongoing medical care for chronic health conditions, etc.

6) Your Living Situation: Where you will live, how long you can live there, how you will support yourself, a realistic budget, etc.

7) Personal Support: A) Your support network. B) Letters from your family and others with details about how they can support you.

8) Potential Problems with Compliance: How will you ensure compliance with parole requirements, treatment, job expectations, medications, and so forth?

9) Potential Problems With Stress and Coping: A) How will you cope with stress and difficult situations? B) Do you have a spiritual practice or other means of stress reduction, anger management techniques, support groups, family and friends?

10) Solid, Realistic, Certain, Clear: Be sure your parole plans are solid and realistic; A) The Board can and does sometimes check on letters of support and offers of assistance. B) By being specific and clear, you prevent the Board from discounting your plans because they are vague or not verifiable. Of course, it is very difficult to predict what someone is going to be doing several years in the future, or to present concrete job offers, but it is useful for you to gather as much specific information as possible. You should highlight any pre-prison job experience, in-prison job experience, job training, and education.

You will have to show why your living environment will be safe, stable, and crime-free if you're released. If you have frequent visits or communication with family or friends, this should also be brought up.

CHAPTER 5

Your Attorney's Role

As a Lifer candidate for parole, you are entitled by law to the assistance of an attorney to help you prepare for your hearing, and to represent you at the hearing. Good legal counsel can increase your chances of attaining parole; a trained and experienced attorney is especially needed for the hearing, as thorough preparation and investigation, good coaching, proper objections, complete and frank presentation of your case, careful questioning to provide clarity, and a motivating closing statement are all critically important. If you do not or cannot hire a private attorney, the Board will appoint one for you. These attorneys are not slaves to the Board, but they aren't paid very much and, of course, their experience varies. Some of the Board's attorneys are very good indeed, but your assignment will be by the luck of the draw – so, if you and your family can afford to hire an attorney, strongly consider it. Either way, once you have your attorney, you and your attorney must work closely together and do every single thing you can think of to show the Board that you are suitable for parole.

The Board Packet

The coordinator of Lifer hearings at the prison where you are housed will provide your attorney with a set of documents called the "Board Packet"; this contains the main documents that will be considered by the Board at the hearing. Your attorney should supplement the material in the Board Packet by obtaining other documents from your Central File and from your family and friends. Your attorney should not assume the Board Packet has all the documents necessary to prepare for a hearing.

Board Packets are due for delivery approximately 60 days prior to the scheduled hearing date. This allows enough time for you and your attorney to review the packet and determine whether documents are missing, and whether you should request a postponement, stipulation, or waiver.

The subsections here below describe the materials that are generally included in the Board Packet.

A) Checklist: The Packet should contain a checklist (inventory) of all the documents that should be in the Packet. You or your attorney must confirm you received the documents that are checked on the list. If all the documents were not provided and your attorney needs more time, your attorney should consider objecting, or requesting a postponement or continuance, until the missing documents can be supplied.

B) Cumulative Case Summary: The Packet should contain a chronological history of every transfer or major classification change in your institutional history, including any changes in your parole date. It also documents each parole hearing and its outcome.

C) Board Reports: The Packet should contain all your Life Prisoner Evaluation Reports that have been completed. Prior to each parole hearing, a Correctional Counselor reviews the Central File and writes a report about what you have done good and bad – since your last parole hearing. This is known as the "Board Report." There should also be a summary of all previous disciplinary violations, and of your self-help, educational, and vocational programs. These reports often omit both your recent and your old accomplishments; for this reason, you and/or your attorney should bring any significant certificates or chronos to the hearing.

D) Notices and Responses: This section will contain all of your letters of support received for your upcoming hearing. In addition, there will be copies of the notices that the Board sends out prior to each hearing to let the victim, victim's family, prosecutor, police, and sentencing judge know of the upcoming parole hearing, and inviting them to provide input. If any written opposition (or support) is submitted by any of these individuals, it will be found here. If any support letters are not in this section of the Packet, you or your attorney should bring those letters to the hearing and/or attach them to any Hearing Memorandum (more on this below).

E) Legal Documents: The documents in this section include the Probation Officer's Report (POR), which is the most common source for the Statement of Facts relied on by the panel at a parole hearing. The section may also include important statements made by witnesses or codefendants, as well as your statements made shortly after the crime or after arrest. The Abstract of Judgment showing your sentence will be in this section, as well as any

Appellate Court decision following any appeal of the conviction. Sometimes sentencing transcripts will also be included. It is important for you and your attorney to pay special attention to this section prior to the initial parole consideration hearing, because that hearing "sets" the Statement of Facts that will be used in future hearings and provides the best opportunity to set the record straight on descriptions of the crime or other facts that may be incorrect in the POR or other documents.

F) Confidential Information: There will be no confidential information in the Packet. There may be documents in your Central File that are not provided to you or your attorney for safety or security reasons. Confidential information typically involves codefendants, gang affiliations, or similarly sensitive matters. At the beginning of the parole hearing, the panel members will inform you if any of the confidential information will be used in their consideration of your suitability for parole.

Review Entire Central File

The Board hearing panel members do not always review your entire Central Vile prior to the hearing, although the File is usually brought to the hearing room. The information in your Central File is much more extensive than the materials provided to your attorney in the Board Packet. Therefore, your attorney should review your entire Central File to find all possible material that could show that you are suitable for parole. Otherwise, the Board may not be aware of all the information that is in your Central File. It's important that your attorney introduce and discuss all beneficial file documents at the hearing and in the written statement. Your attorney should also take note of, and object to the consideration of, any material that the prison staff themselves have deemed unreliable.

You and your attorney can arrange to review your Central File. This can usually be done through your Correctional Counselor, although staff at the "Lifer Desk" will sometimes arrange these reviews. Your attorney is entitled to review and receive copies of any materials within the Central File, except materials specifically withheld as "confidential."

The Central File usually contains documents regarding the criminal offense, including:

1) The Criminal Complaint, Information, or Indictment;
2) Transcripts of the hearings on Entry of the Plea and/or Sentencing; Pre-sentencing or Probation Reports;

Any correspondence pertaining to the case from defense counsel, the judge, the District Attorney's office, and other persons who have submitted views pursuant to Penal Code § 3043.5.

Other sections of the Central File contain "chronos," or short documents written by custodial, educational, psychological, and vocational staff. It is fairly common for laudatory chronos to appear in a prisoner's file documenting good job or school performance, or other positive programming efforts. Your attorney should review these chronos thoroughly and obtain copies of helpful or harmful chronos for presentation or response.

Another section of the File will contain disciplinary reports and counseling chronos documenting your misconduct or rule violations. Copies of these reports and chronos should be obtained by your attorney, as they will need to be addressed at the hearing. Your attorney should also obtain copies of classification chronos regarding Security Housing placement for non-disciplinary reasons such as alleged gang affiliation, protective needs, psychiatric needs, management problems, or suspected improper behavior.

Written Hearing Memorandum

Since Lifers and their attorneys are not usually permitted to make an opening statement at the hearing, your attorney may want to prepare a written hearing brief, or Memorandum. Your attorney can send three copies of the Memorandum to the Board Lifer Desk or to the Classification and Parole Representative (C&PR) at the institution where the hearing is to be held. Sent on time, the Board will see the Memorandum before the hearing and be better prepared for your attorney's presentation. If not sent on time, the Memorandum can also be presented to the panel at the time of the hearing, probably with reduced effectiveness.

A suggested format is to set forth an introduction in which the Lifer's strongest points and overall theme are presented, followed by sections that address the issues of suitability, recommended release date, and post-conviction credits. If you have had prior suitability hearings, your attorney should address the issues that arose at those hearings and state what you have done to fulfill the prior panels' recommendations. If your attorney is going to present live testimony or documentary evidence at the hearing, brief summaries of these materials should be included in the written statement. Any additional written materials you wish the panel to consider should be discussed in and attached to the Memorandum.

Hearing Participants

At least 30 days before the hearing, the Board sends notices about the hearing to many people, including victim or victim's next of kin, your trial attorney, the District Attorney and the police investigators who were involved in your prosecution, and the judge who sentenced you. These parties will be invited to either attend the hearing or submit written or recorded statements.

There are other parties who are not invited to attend parole hearings, but who are specifically invited to provide written comments in support of or in Opposition to your parole. These parties include the judge of the Superior Court of conviction, the attorney who represented you at trial, and the law enforcement agency that investigated the case. You and your attorney should receive copies of any statements submitted by the prosecutor, judges, or police.

Prisoner Testimony

Lifers have the right to speak on their own behalf and to ask and answer questions at the hearing. It is a violation of Due Process if a prisoner is not allowed to appear before the Board and present evidence. In other words, you clearly have a right to testify at the parole hearing.

However, you and your attorney must give careful consideration to whether or not you should testify or answer questions from the hearing panel. Factors to be weighted include whether your version of the crime is the same as that in the File, whether there is information in the File to support your version, and what impression you may make while testifying. If you maintain your innocence or have a totally different view of the facts, your testimony may create more questions than answers. Also, you may agree to discuss other matters but refuse to discuss the facts of the crime. The refusal may not legally be held against you, but direct testimony can create rapport between you and the panel, and may remind the panel that you're a real human being. Generally, unless there is a clear reason not to testify, you should testify and be prepared to answer difficult questions.

Favorable Witnesses

Your attorney should also attempt to find witnesses favorable to you and get statements from them. Your attorney should interview witnesses who can offer favorable information on any part of your life, commitment offense, or other crimes. For example, your attorney may want to contact the authors of any favorable documents in your Central File and obtain from them, if possible, a verbal or a written statement that they do not see you, if released, as a danger to society. It may also be worthwhile for your attorney to interview the victim of the crime, or the victim's next of kin, who may be willing in some cases to give a statement indicating a lack of opposition to parole. However, your attorney must be very careful not to cause additional stress or harm to the victim or the victim's family.

Testimony of favorable witnesses can also be presented to the hearing panel in the form of letters and declarations, which ideally should be signed under penalty of perjury. Cooperative witnesses should be asked to prepare written statements to be submitted as part of the written Memorandum or at the time of the hearing if no Memorandum is submitted in advance.

In many things in life you have to do your best to succeed, but at the same time prepare for failure and the next step. So it is at a parole hearing: you will prepare diligently, rehearse, write, show up, and do your part. Expectations are high (and should be; parole rates are rising and you have an excellent case). Yet, you may be denied, in spite of all that. So, what's next?

Well, there may be no "next", unless your attorney has already done his "other" job – preserving the issues for later appeal (to the Board, or by habeas petition). This will be important even if you are granted parole, because the full Board or Governor can cause the grant to be rescinded. This preservation is usually done by your attorney's making of objections during the hearing (by the way, you can object, too, even against the advice or forgetfulness of your attorney).

As the hearing begins, the Commissioner will actually invite objections. Your attorney should make good use of your document review, objecting to the use of any unfavorable document that can be impeached, to every disciplinary action with mitigating factors, and so on. The attorney should object to use of the nature of the crime, as being too long ago to matter. The attorney should object to any negative finding in the psychological evaluation.

As the hearing progresses, your attorney should object to certain questions, such as those that might incriminate you, or about subjects you've already told the Board you won't discuss, or that are hounding or intimidating. Objections also go against questionable evidence, against hearsay, against unsupported conclusions, against confidential information not covered by a Form 1030. The attorney will likely save some or all of his or her objections until the closing statement, so as not to annoy the panel, but certainly in the closing statement your attorney must object to misinformation and bias in the preceding remarks by the District Attorney, and to certain remarks by the panel during the hearing.

The panel discourages commentary during the Decision portion of the hearing, considering it merely an announcement. Nevertheless, if the panel has abused the process (for example, by citing reasons not discussed during the hearing), or shows extreme bias or plain error, your attorney should attempt to object. Even if rebuffed, those few words in the record will be important later.

It's unfortunate that your attorney, at least, has to handle this extra duty, and you'll need to pay some attention; try to let him or her handle it all, so you can just deal with the questions. The subject can't be covered here, but without these preparations, you might not have a case to take to a court about your denial. So, plan your hearing strategy with your attorney, then work hard to not need later any of the objections that get made, by getting a grant.

CHAPTER 6

Earning a Parole Date

Previous chapters have no doubt shown you that preparing for your parole hearing takes dedicated personal effort, and that the Board is looking for real and sustained rehabilitation; it's not a walk-through where you pick up a ticket – you will have to earn your parole date. To earn your parole date, there are many things you will have to do: Take every class and program that you can. Read books, and write book reports on each one. Join available groups at your prison, and get involved with all self-help that will help you with personal growth or give you opportunities to help others. Stay in contact or get in contact with healthy family and friends on the outside. Limit your contact with negative people on the inside. Think about who you are and who you want to be. Make sure you keep track of all your positive work and behavior so you can talk about it at your hearing. Prepare and present your parole plans for when you get out.

The Requirements for a Parole Date

To obtain a parole date through the Board, you must normally, among other things, comply with each and every one of the following general requirements. If any one item is missing, then it is very unlikely that a parole date will be granted. There are two parts to these requirements that you will need to satisfy: "Inside" and "Outside" Requirements.

"Inside" Requirements for a Parole Date

"Inside" requirements are documents pertaining to your conduct during the period of incarceration (post-conviction factors):

1) EDUCATION. You shall acquire a GED, or a High School Diploma. Proof of the GED or High School Diploma must be placed in your C-File. Additional advanced formal education is also positively regarded but not required.

2) VOCATION. You shall complete a certified vocation within your institution or institutions while incarcerated. Multiple vocations are highly regarded, and should be sought if possible.

3) SELF-HELP. It is highly recommended that you regularly attend some form of self-help counseling. Typically, AA or NA, or other programs, may be available. In addition to attending, you should demonstrate knowledge of the concepts taught in the programs attended. If you attend either AA or NA, you should be knowledgeable in the 12 Steps. It is common for members of the panel to inquire of you about what steps are most important, and how the steps are applied in daily life. Do not think that you need not attend self-help groups, such as AA or NA, simply because you never had an alcohol or drug problem. Attendance is recommended for all inmates, regardless of personal history.

4) WRITTEN PAROLE PLANS. You should present letters of support to the Board at the parole hearing. The letters should be dated within six months of the hearing. Older letters should be updated with a new letter indicating that the information in the old letter is still current and valid. You should have a letter indicating that "In the event a parole

date is granted for the inmate, he is invited to live with me." In other words, the letter should indicate an offer of housing. Multiple offers of support are always advantageous.

The second aspect of good parole plans is a job offer upon release. The job offer should preferably be in the same geographic area as any offers of residential support.

If you have an INS hold and anticipate being deported to another country, you will still need to present parole plans for your state in the form of an offer of residence and an offer of employment. If you expect to be deported to another country you will probably need to present at least two sets of parole plans – one for your state and a second set of plans for the country of eventual deportation.

5) PSYCHOLOGICAL REPORT. You should have a recent positive psychological evaluation. It is very difficult to set forth descriptions of what constitutes a positive report. Each report must be evaluated on a case by case basis. It is preferable that you have at least two positive reports from different professionals. Remember that the attorney must request a new psychological report at the parole hearing. If neither your attorney nor the Board on its own motion requests a new report, none will be prepared for the next suitability hearing.

6) DISCIPLINARY HISTORY. You should be disciplinary free for at least five to ten years before any parole hearing in which you expect to get a parole date.

In addition, it is very hard for dates to be given to those who have a Level IV classification score or are housed at a maximum security prison. So, it is important that you try to reach lower level prisons. The negative impact of even a single disciplinary conviction cannot be stressed enough. Avoid them at all costs, if at all possible.

"Outside" Requirements for a Parole Date

"Outside" requirements are documents pertaining to parole plans upon release:

1) PICTURES TO SUPPORT EMPLOYMENT OFFERS. These must be dated within the previous six months before your hearing. If you have a family business to step back into, show a picture of your family standing in front of the business. If you have a job offer from an employer, show a picture of the employer's business properties. Make your opportunities real to the Commissioner by showing photos of those people, businesses, and places. Otherwise, the only real thing is your C-File and you – alone in your prison wardrobe sitting in front of the panel.

2) DOCUMENTS PERTAINING TO TRANSPORTATION RESOURCES. If you have a spouse, or relative, or friend with a car, show a photocopy of the registration and insurance, along with the letter promising use of the car. Convince the Commissioners that you will have transportation available to you.

3) HOUSING. Include photographs of the family home, or the home where you will be provided housing. If you will be expected to enter into some sort of halfway use, include letters from that facility to show that you have been in contact with them recently, and everything is in order for you to enter when you get out of prison.

4) WHY HAVE A PACKAGE THAT YOU PRESENT TO THE BOARD? Because humans learn through their EYES much more than through their EARS. Nothing is real to most people until you SHOW THEM (eyes). When you sitting in front of the Commissioners in a hearing but do not have a package speaking for you – something for them to look at – you are at the terrible disadvantage of convincing someone with your words (their ears) instead of with pictures (their eyes). Don't make that mistake. Remember the old saying, "A picture is worth a thousand words." Why? Because we are visual creatures.

Things to Remember

1) The Board regards the lack of disciplinary violations as a gauge to evaluate whether you have matured enough to follow the rules and regulations of society. Lack of disciplinary write-ups means that you have learned to control your emotions in situations where in the past you would have impulsively acted out; it shows restraint. If you have any disciplinary violations since your last hearing, you will face probable denial of a date. Again, the negative impact of even a single disciplinary write-up cannot be stressed strongly enough.

2) Review your C-File prior to the hearing. Make sure all of your positive documents are there.

3) If you have a clean record, if your crime is not too horrifying to the average reader (Commissioner, or Deputy Commissioner), then you need to focus on education, trades, psychological reports, and parole plans. With your parole plans, it will be helpful to have your supporting family and friends provide some details. For example, regarding housing: Will you be provided with a room? Help with food? A car? Regarding a job: How much will you be paid? How many hours a week? Help with transportation to and from work?

4) Never forget that all of these steps are a long-term requirement. This is a long-term plan – years if you get to the point where you are getting three-year denials ... don't get discouraged. You may be getting close. Do not think that you have automatically reached the finish line complying with Board requests over a span of a year from your last hearing. You will almost certainly need to demonstrate self-discipline over time, and persevere in the face of adversity.

5) Show self-help, even if there are no current programs available to you in the institution. Think innovatively. Read

books about self-improvement, religion, and psychology – whatever your interests may be – and document your readings. Write about what you have read. Documenting books that you read shows self-help as well as advancement of your education. It also demonstrates your willingness to take that extra step. Keep a record of all the books that you have read, and bring that written record to each of your parole hearings.

What Is the Board Looking For?

The easy answer is that the Board wants to make sure that it does not release someone who will commit another crime. This core determination is an assessment of your current dangerousness. But you cannot simply tell the Board that you do not want to come back to prison, or that you will not commit another crime. Your words are not enough. You must SHOW the Board that you will not commit crimes in the future. There are two steps to doing so:

Step One: Explain your understanding of why you committed your crime (you cannot do this if you deny your crime, minimize your role in the crime, or blame others). You need to show documents or statements pertaining to the crime.

1) Statements of remorse.

2) Demonstrate profound character development and insight into the crime. Even if drugs or alcohol weren't involved in the crime (and especially if they were), show a continuous pattern of AA and NA participation for your entire time incarcerated. Make contacts on the outside for AA or NA support, such as a sponsor. Also attend any and all other self-help groups offered, and keep ALL your certificates and documents.

Step Two: Show BY YOUR ACTIONS how you've developed into a different person today compared to when you committed the crime. You'll need documents pertaining to conduct during the period of incarceration.

1) GED or High School Diploma, or college credit course completed. If you don't have a GED or High School Diploma, focus first on attaining one or the other. If you do have one or the other, get enrolled in college courses as soon as possible.

2) Certificates of completion of vocational training. See what your prison offers and do what you can to be placed in a vocation. Ask your Correctional Counselor to put you on the waiting list.

3) Laudatory chronos.

4) Resumé.

5) Certificates of attendance at AA, NA, and whatever other self-help programs you have attended.

6) Summary of lack of disciplinary violations.

If you do not show with your actions that you are now a different person and demonstrate that you understand what led up to your involvement in the crime, the Board will not believe that you can prevent it from happening again.

Also, even though it's well known to the inmate population that getting assigned to education, vocational training, jobs, and even self-help groups is out of your hands, it's not well known to the Board. An inmate can sit in a cell unassigned anywhere from months to years, even though the inmate wants to get assigned and participate. But the Board won't understand that, and if you try to tell them it's out of your hands, they'll consider it an excuse.

So, this is how you combat that problem to the best of your ability – SHOW that you were actually trying to get assigned and participate: Once a month, fill out a couple "Inmate Requests"; address one to your Correctional Counselor, and the other to Assignments. On the "Inmate Requests," ask to be assigned to any available education, vocational trades, jobs, and self-help groups. Send in the requests and keep your copies and any replies for your file. That way, you at least have documentation that you've tried.

When Should I Start Preparing for My Hearing?

"NOW!" The Board considers your entire time in prison in deciding whether to grant parole, or not. Focus on the present and use the time in a way that will help you get ready to go home. It is never too early to start preparing, but it is also never too late. Even if you were not on the right track before, you can turn things around and show the Board you are ready to go home.

How Can I Start Preparing for My Parole Hearing?

Here are some starter questions to help you begin thinking deeply about some of the issues the Board will want you to address.

Take your time on these: COMMITMENT OFFENSE what was going through my mind as I made the choices that led to my committing the crime? Why did I not stop the crime from happening? How would I handle the same situation differently today?

How were my victim(s) hurt? What did they feel? How were their family members and friends affected at the time of the crime? How was the community affected? And now, years later, what is the impact of what I did?

SOCIAL HISTORY

How were my relationships with my family members? Who were my role models?

What did they teach me (good and bad)? Prior to my crime, did I experience, violence, abuse (physical, sexual, verbal, emotional), neglect, poverty, mental illness, drug use, gangs, or criminal activity in my family? How did that affect me (anger, denial, loneliness, low self-esteem)? What decisions did I make about who I wanted to be (or not be) when I got older? How did my experiences in my family and community impact my decisions? What is different now? How did I get from there to here?

Did you use drugs or alcohol? Can I remember the first time? What was the situation? Did my drug or alcohol use begin (or increase) because I was experiencing some other difficulty that I did not know how to deal with? What is different now? How did I get from there to here?

Were you associated with gangs? When did I start to get involved? What did I think gangs would give me that was missing in my life? What was my experience with gangs? What did I believe about gangs. How was my gang involvement related to things going on in my family, community, or school? What is different now? How did I get from there to here?

Did you sell drugs or commit other crimes? When did I start doing this, and why? How did it make me feel? How   was my criminal behavior related to things going on in my family, community or school? What is different now?

POST-COMMITMENT

Did you have a negative disciplinary record in prison? What was going on in my life that I chose to do things that would get me in trouble in prison? What is different now? What types of programs have I participated in while in prison to better myself? What were one or two programs that really focused on addressing my specific needs? What specific tools have I gained from these programs? What led me to violate the rules of the prison? Do I take responsibility for those violations? How will I avoid violating rules if I am released?

CHAPTER 7

Youth Offender Hearings

In 2014, Senate Bill 260 created special Youth Offender Parole Hearings (also called "SB 260 Hearings") for prisoners who are serving long indeterminate (life with the possibility of parole) or determinate (set-length) terms for crimes they committed when they were under the age of 18. In October 2015, SB 261 expanded these parole hearings to include prisoners who committed their crimes when they were ages 18 through 22. As of October 2017, Assembly Bill 1308 expands Youth Offender parole Hearings to include prisoners who committed their crimes when they were 25 or younger. Additionally, SB 394 mades some youth-offender prisoners eligible even though sentenced to Life Without Parole (LWOP), namely those convicted of crimes committed when they were under the age of 18, and who have served at least 25 years. These two most recent laws took effect on January 1, 2018.

The Youth Offender Parole Law

The Youth Offender Parole Law is set forth in Penal Code (PC) §§ 3051, 3051.1, and 4801. Youth Offender Parole Hearings are held after the prisoner has served either 15, 20, or 25 years of incarceration, depending on the type of sentence they are serving. The Hearings take into consideration the fact that youth are less responsible for their actions than are adults; the features of youth (for example, that youth are not as good as adults at understanding the risk and consequences of their actions, at resisting impulse and peer pressure, or at controlling their surroundings); and any rehabilitation and increased maturity over time.

The law includes deadlines by which the Board must have completed hearings for everyone who is eligible and who already has served enough time to get a Youth Offender Parole Hearing. The deadlines depend on a prisoner's age at the time of the crime and what type of sentence they are serving. If you were 25 or younger at the time of your crime, you should have a "Youth Offender Parole Hearing." The purpose of the Youth Offender Parole Hearing (YOPH) is to decide if you are suitable for parole and to "provide a meaningful opportunity to obtain release." PC 3015(a)(1) & (e). This means the law gives you a real chance of getting out of prison on parole, because of the characteristics of your youth that would not have been considered at a regular parole hearing; you and many other prisoners will also get an earlier opportunity to earn parole and get out of prison.

How Will a YOPH Be Different From a Regular Parole Hearing?

The Board Commissioners must now consider qualified youth offenders differently from someone who was 26 or older at the time of their crime. The fact that you were young at the time of the crime should count as one reason in favor of granting you parole. Though you still have to work hard to show that you would not pose a danger to the community if released, the YOPH process should increase your chance of being paroled. PC 3051(d).

On the one hand, many things about a YOPH are the same as a regular parole hearing. For example, you will still have to be found suitable for parole in order to be released, and the suitability and unsuitability factors remain the same. You will have the right to an attorney, and all other rights you would have at a regular parole hearing.

But, YOPH5 should also be very different because the Board must give "great weight" to: the fact that youth are less responsible than adults for their actions (the "Diminished Culpability" of youth); the Hallmark Features of youth (for example, that youth are, as compared to adults, not as good at understanding the risks and consequences of their actions or at resisting impulse and peer pressure, and are less in control of their life circumstances; etc.); and any subsequent growth and increased maturity of the prisoner. PC 4801 (c).

If you already had a parole hearing before the Youth Offender Parole Law went into effect, your next parole hearing will be a YOPH.

What is a YPED, MEPD, or EPRD?

YPED stands for "Youth Parole Eligibility Date"; it is the amount of time an eligible youth offender must serve before having his or her first Youth Offender Parole Hearing. In other words, it is the date that a person is eligible for release if found suitable for parole at a Youth Offender Parole Hearing.

The date of your YPED is set by the Youth Offender Parole Law. PC 3051(b). Your YPED will be the first day of your 15th, 20th, or 25th year of incarceration (which means after you have served 14, 19, or 24 years). All of the time that you have been in custody on your case – including a juvenile facility, jail, in prison, mental health facility, and at DJJ or CYA – counts toward your years of incarceration.

MEDP stands for "Minimum Eligible Parole Date"; it is the amount of time that a person with a life sentence must serve before having his or her first parole hearing. Everyone who has a life sentence (other than Life Without the Possibility of Parole) has a MEDP. A person who qualified for Youth Offender Parole may have both a YPED and A MEPD.

EPRD means "Earliest Possible Release Date"; it is the amount of time a person with a determinate sentence (nonlife sentence) serves before being released. A person who qualifies for Youth Offender Parole and does not have a life sentence may have both a YPED and an EPRD.

As far as when your first YOPH parole hearing will be: the one that matters is the one that is earliest. If your YEPD is before your MEPD, then your YPED determines when your hearing will be set, and the reverse is true: if your MEPD is earlier, then the MEPD determines your hearing date and possibility for release. The same is true for an EPRD and YPED: whichever is earlier is the one that will determine when your first hearing is held, or when you are released.

Controlling Offense

If you are eligible for Youth Offender Parole, your "Controlling Offense" determines when your YPED is. The controlling offense is the one with the longest single term; it is the sentence for a single count or enhancement for which you received the longest term of imprisonment. PC 3051 (a)(2)(B).

Think about your sentence and the different terms that make up the whole sentence. For example, if you have a 30-to-life sentence, it is really several terms that add up to 30-to-life. It could be two 15-to-life sentences, or 5 years with a 25-to-life enhancement, or some other combination. The longest individual term determines your YPED.

If you have more than one sentence, you will have a YOPH at the time set by your YPED and, if granted parole, you will immediately be eligible for release. You do not have to serve other consecutive sentences or enhancements related to your controlling offense. PC 3046(c).

If Granted Parole, When Will I Be Released?

The Board has up to 120 days to review and finalize the panel's Decision to grant parole. You will be notified if the Board makes any changes to the Decision that adversely affect you. If the Board does not change its mind in the 120 days, the Decision goes to the governor's office for review.

The State constitution allows the governor to affirm, modify, or reverse the Board's Decision to grant parole in the following cases. Cal. Constitution Art. 5, Sec. 8(b). If you have a life sentence for murder, the governor can reverse the Board's decision to grant or deny parole. The governor has up to 30 days to review the Board's Decision. In non-murder cases, the governor cannot reverse the Board's Decision, but he can require the full Board to reconsider the Decision and potentially change the Decision.

If the governor decides to take no action in your case, you will be released. Do I Have to Serve My "Thompson Term"?

Maybe not. If you have been convicted and sentenced for new crimes committed before age 26 (during your incarceration), often called "Thompson terms," you might not be required to serve the sentences for these crimes after you are found suitable for Youth Offender Parole.

In April 2017, the California Court of Appeal, First Appellate District, decided In re Trejo, 10 Cal.App.5th 972 (2017), which held that PC 3051 (the Youth Offender Parole Law, requiring youth offenders to be released once they have reached their YPED and been found suitable) supersedes PC 1170.1 (requiring that an inmate sentenced to consecutive terms not be released on parole before completing all the terms of imprisonment imposed).

At this time, CDCR and the Board are requiring people to serve "Thompson terms" for offenses committed after age 25. Many people are challenging this interpretation of Trejo in court, and some people have won these cases.

I Was Denied Parole. Now What?

Your next hearing will be scheduled according to "Marsy's Law," which was enacted in 2008. At the end of the hearing, the Commissioners will decide whether your next parole hearing will be in 3, 5, 7, 10, or 15 years. In making that determination, the Youth Offender Parole Laws require the Commissioners to consider the same factors as in the parole grant/deny determination, namely, that you were under the age of 26 at the time of the crime, the diminished culpability of youth as compared to that of adults, the hallmark features of youth, and any subsequent growth and increased maturity of the individual. PC 305 1(g).

If you were denied parole, but have a determinate sentence and your EPRD is before your next parole hearing, you will be released at the EPRD established on the determinate term. You do not have to wait until your next parole hearing.

If you want to challenge your parole denial in the first 120 days after the Decision, you can send a letter to the Board's Decision Review Board. After 150 days, you can file a petition for a Writ of Habeas Corpus asking a judge to review the Board's denial (or the Governor's reversal) of parole.

Remember that laws change, and before relying on anything in this chapter you should make sure you have the most up-to-date information on the laws. Is There a Role for Family and Friends?

Yes, there is a special role at the Youth Offender Parole Hearing regarding friends and family members. The Youth

Offender Parole Laws state that family members, friends, school personnel, faith leaders, and representatives from community-based organizations who have knowledge about the young person prior to the crime, or who can attest to his or her growth and maturity since the time of the crime, can submit letters to the Board. This is allowed in regular parole hearings, as well, but the fact that the Youth Offender Law specifically includes this should make the Commissioners pay extra attention to that support for youth offenders. This law does not, however, allow friends and family to come to the hearing. PC 3051 (17)(2).

PART TWO:

Understanding Recidivism

The information in Part Two was inspired by and is credited to the writings of Clarence A. Taylor.

Any person sitting in a prison cell that has already reoffended and returned to prison for a subsequent term should not take recidivism for granted. It is the real situation of over half the incarcerated people in America. There are over two million incarcerated recidivist offenders, many already three-strike felons. Any person sitting in a prison cell that is in his or her first term should face those facts with alarm, and not take lightly their own chances for return to prison, and seek diligently to lower those chances drastically. Part Two is here to help you confront and uproot the deep-seated compulsive nature that causes recidivism.

CHAPTER 8

Challenges To Face and Overcome

The truth is, most recidivists are completely baffled about the overwhelming forces that make them repeat the same cycle over and over. The want to change; they want to redeem themselves, but all they have thought and tried seems to fail. It is time to enter the abyss and to acknowledge the deeper, darker, reality that repeated criminal behavior is linked in many ways to unconscious psychological and emotional dynamics. It is linked to a compelling urge to indiscriminately meet one or more basic psycho-social needs that are partly or completely unsatisfied in a person who, for some reason, has not learned how to, or felt able to, fulfill those needs in a healthy, conventional way. If you can't summon the strength and courage to face the labor of transformation; if you don't have the willingness to suffer for your freedom; then freedom will not be in you. And without freedom within there can definitely be none without.

Transformation of the Compulsive-Criminal Mentality

It is an error of grave consequence for compulsive offenders and society to believe that transformation of the compulsive-criminal mentality is as simple as making a choice or decision to go straight, or then to believe that a G.E.D. or vocational certificate will redeem the character. For the compulsive criminal, education and vocational goals are goals to be achieved during the process of uprooting the mentality. They are not a means to that end.

In order to transform the compulsive-criminal mentality you have to uproot the deep-seated emotions and beliefs that it its compulsive nature. While incarcerated, these forces are usually dormant. That's how so many people end up neglecting to confront the root of their compulsive criminality, and then find out shortly after release that it is still very active, i.e., that even they themselves have been deluded by the illusion of change. Some people can stop compulsive behavior through their resolve to exercise willpower, but most can't. They need understanding, counseling, encouragement, and emotional insights. They need some form of analysis of what is causing them to be compulsive. They need to summon the courage to look within the depths of themselves, because as long as they stay on the surface, they will remain largely in the dark, and continue to chase a phantom.

It is up to the citizens and perpetrators to get a real understanding and start the dialogue to change this. The system doesn't care. In fact, the system has an interest in crime and recidivism. Look at all the people who are employed in criminal law and corrections. Look at all the expansion of "prison industrial complexes" and private ownership of prison operations that involve money. A collect call from prison is four hundred percent more costly than the same call at the same distance outside a prison. American corporations have made a business of profiting from crime. But this is nothing surprisingly new; crime has always paid someone substantial sums – it just hasn't been the victims or perpetrators. The system will never seriously challenge the causes of recidivism, any more than it challenges the causes of poverty and homelessness.

It's up to you. Only you can truly transform yourself! Overcoming Recidivism

You are only going to overcome recidivism by perceiving, acknowledging, and understanding the truth about yourself:

1) There are specific condition within your personality that influence you to commit criminal acts, or use substances that can result in your incarceration because they are illegal to possess.

2) These conditions are most likely related to deficiencies in your human constitution; that is, basic needs have not been healthily and genuinely fulfilled. To begin with, self-esteem, self-acceptance, self-determination, self-love, self-understanding, self-knowledge, etc., are involved in how one relates to himself or herself and are of primary importance. They are needs as basic to the mind, soul, and psyche as vitamin A is to the proper development of eyesight, or vitamin C is to skeletal formation.

A lack of self-esteem undermines the degree to which you are self-accepting, thereby making it difficult to be self-forgiving, which weighs heavily against one's ability to genuinely fulfill other basic needs. All of these basic psycho-social needs have a function within the totality of what it means to be human. They are links in a chain, but much more intricately interconnected.

But when it comes to recidivism, it is vital to understand these interconnections because the degree of their wellbeing determines the overall social well-being of the individual. Understand this reality, that whenever basic psycho-social needs (mental, emotional, psychological, spiritual) are unfulfilled, their inescapable importance will compel and drive the mind to search for and pursue pathological methods of artificial achievement or fulfillment. The individual, however, will not perceive that those methods - by which he or she is compulsively tying to fulfill the basic needs through compensation – are artificial and, ultimately, unfulfilling.

The only way to free oneself from recidivism is to uproot the conditions in one's mind that make recidivism possible. What, then, one has to ask, are these conditions? To begin with, recidivism is perpetuated by the condition of self-condemnation because of one's past criminal act(s) or behavior(s). Once you judge yourself with condemnation, you undermine your ability to be genuinely self-forgiving. You have a need, despite society's attitudes, to forgive yourself. If you do not, then you are also a prisoner to an unconscious form of internal oppression.

Overcoming recidivism is not a matter of achieving external, social goals, but more one of freeing oneself from internal conditions that have been repressed and are unconsciously driving the mind, emotions, and will. This must be understood.

The Unconscious (Subconscious)

The unconscious mind is an area that we can access through complete and unreserved expression and can bring things up from, but it's not an area that we can control and edit like the conscious. Therefore, any feelings, anxieties, or fears that we push into the unconscious are out of our reach in terms of turning them off and on, or regulating them. In the unconscious they generally become our master, and while we are hardly aware of their true power, they compel us to act in ways that we often feel unable to control or understand.

While these feelings, anxieties, and fears that we have repressed in order to cope with life lurk like tyrants in the subconscious, they torment our conscious lives with all sorts of compulsive behavior, depending on who we are. Some people feel driven to eat themselves into obesity and poor health. Others feel driven to use narcotics, or to commit crimes for something. There are many forms of behavior that are destructive to our lives, yet we may feel unable to stop the behavior. But – what is it that really keeps us from stopping or controlling these self-destructive behaviors is that for the most part we refuse to become conscious of the repressed (hidden) feelings that influence them.

As long as they are repressed, they have pathological control over us. But when we develop the strength to consciously feel and experience them, we have the opportunity to take control and do what we want with them. The point is not to avoid them, but to face them in order to transform them, thereby uprooting the conditions that bring our self-defeating attitudes and behavior into being, including compulsive criminality.

It is up to each individual who has had difficulty understanding the causes of his problems in the past and now to do an honest self-evaluation of himself or herself, to pinpoint the problems and set out upon a real, constructive path to overcoming the internal and external difficulties. This begins for you when you first accept yourself as worthy of any and all effort you can put forward to overcome the compulsive criminal mentality and any other form of reactionary, compulsive behavior.

Moral Values

Does having a criminal history mean that you're an immoral person? All that I know and understand about human behavior, social law, and morality leads me to believe that everyone has morals. The question then becomes: How does one's moral integrity break down? Or, to what degree of expression do one's moral values conform to or restrict behavior in relation to healthy living and social interaction?

A man may be a merciless robber, yet at the same time have strong moral restraints within him against rape and the burglary of private homes. So, what are the emotional and psychological factors that allow him to be totally against one type of committing harm to others, yet not all types in general? To answer this question, the individual has to find out to what degree he is undernourished in the satisfaction of his own basic psycho-social needs. That is, how severe is the absence of fulfillment of certain emotional and psychological necessities within his character, necessities such as a sense of value, personal power, self-confidence, etc.? Again, the greater the degree of absence, the stronger can be the force of sociopathic influences in the person's feelings, thinking, and actions. Therefore, the stronger will be the characteristics within the individual of a pathological, neurotic, criminally compulsive personality.

It is never a simple matter of thinking: This is wrong, so I won't do it. That would be like expecting a starving person to say to himself: "Yes, I'm starving, but it isn't good to eat candy bars and ice cream, so I'll settle for nothing until a healthy meal comes along." No. We have to face reality. When suffering from a starved condition, one is liable to settle as quickly as possible for whatever is available to relieve the hunger, even though he or she knows, as we do, that the contents of the artificial foods will, in the long run, undermine health and longevity.

It's in this sense that the compulsive offender has to understand his criminality.

He is (in his unconscious) very much a starving soul, reaching as compulsively as ever for the most expedient means of quelling his pangs of hunger. The only way to end the hunger and compulsion is to understand and feed with real nutrients the psycho-social necessities of his being. Alcohol, drugs, crime, or loveless sex-crazed relationships will never be genuinely fulfilling. The formula is simple: The greater the degree of real satisfaction of psycho-social needs, then the greater is one's freedom of choice and capacity to maintain a healthy attitude and expression of morality and conduct.

The compulsive repeat offender must make an honest evaluation of his personality conditions. What can be do within his current environment to help himself? He must have the wisdom to acknowledge that he needs as much help as possible, and serious effort is truly required. He cannot expect mere intellectual development to free his mind. He must strive to integrate his thoughts, feelings, and intellect with an emerging new relationship with himself and others. He must become responsible in the sense of knowing his life is solely in his own hands.

CHAPTER 9

Growth and Stagnation

In the book A Psychology of Being, Abraham H. Maslow addressed the question of growth and stagnation, leading up to the point where he states that "Every human being has both sets of forces within him." This simply means that the forces to move ahead as well as those to stand still or move backward exist within each of our personalities. At every point in life and somewhere connected to every decision we make, these two sets of forces are in conflict. Whether we believe this conflict constructively or destructively depends on several possible conditions and attitudes within the personality, and how extreme these conditions and attitudes may be. For example, some of the destructive conditions are of fear, helplessness, insecurity, low self-esteem, and low self-confidence; some of the destructive attitudes are resistance, hostility, vindictiveness, rebellion, and indifference. Each of these personality conditions and attitudes has an influence on the decisions we make in response to life situations.

The Role Feelings Play

As stated by Karen Homey, M.D., in Neurosis and Human Growth, "...It isn't enough to simply think, I lack confidence in myself, or I have a bad temper. You must feel the depth of these conditions within yourself and see the harm they inflict upon your life and personality" (paraphrased). The reason she emphasizes feeling is because thinking, what she calls intellectual realization, "does not take root in us." She says that "What we see with our intellect may be correct, but like a mirror it cannot absorb a ray of light but can only reflect it" (dealing with neuroses).

The typical recidivist has thought, pondered, and intellectually contemplated for years, "Why can't I change and stay out of prison?" But all his efforts to understand and grow have failed. It is necessary to not just think about, but, as Homey advises, feel the reality of ourselves. As she said: "Only then does the force of some unconscious process (and its irrationality) stare us in the face. Only then may we have an incentive to find out more and more about ourselves" (paraphrased).

The character of most men in prison should be rife with conflict between the forces of growth and stagnation, but instead, most seem to have no constructive interest whatsoever in their lives. And even for those who do, seeking education, vocations, and self-teachings, the forces of stagnation still tend to dominate.

So we face the question, why is it so hard for most prisoners to change? What holds them back? How does recidivism become a fate so easily and carelessly accepted?

Each of those questions has to be answered by individuals in relation to themselves and society. But it must be kept in mind that the basic needs -self-acceptance, self-esteem, self-confidence, education, self-actualization, and relationships – should be a starting point in finding your answer. If you identify a deficiency in one or more of these basic needs in yourself, then you need to summon the courage to feel the real impact of these needs not being genuinely fulfilled.

Where does the difficulty lie in "feeling" the depths of basic-needs deficits? Could you temporarily handle feeling no self-esteem or confidence in yourself at all? As a compulsive offender, you probably have a lot of false, neurotic pride, but not an ounce of real confidence. In fact, you probably have the delusion that pride is confidence, which is completely untrue. So the difficulty lies in the dread of bringing to consciousness the feelings of basic anxiety, insecurity, fear, and self-doubt. Questions that you have no firm answer to may arise in your mind, such as, where is my sense of direction? How am I going to face the demands of life as my real self when I'm not sure who I am? What can I do when I have so little knowledge and education? You fear that life may suddenly become an overwhelming phenomenon that literally can or will crush you!

But all these questions and doubts should only be viewed as indicators of where you really need to focus your time and effort. They shouldn't be either avoided or allowed to keep you feeling insecure, though they may temporarily do SO. That is only natural, and not an indication that you are too weak to face life responsibly. You need to have the patience and confidence to build and strengthen yourself in all the ways you need to. You need to tell yourself: "I've got to acknowledge this weakness, and nurture this area of personality, and I'm willing to temporarily experience anxiety, doubt, and, if necessary, pain, to achieve real growth and satisfaction. This is better than spending the rest of my life chasing the ghost of false, temporary relief while revolving in and out of jails and prisons."

Recidivist Tendencies

The truth is that we can hardly ever free ourselves from habitual internal tendencies through the willed suppression of an act or behavior. It is the same with recidivist tendencies. No matter how long we are imprisoned, or how much we are deprived of or restricted in our freedoms, incarceration in and of itself will not free a person from recidivist tendencies, whether it be three years, twenty years, or thirty years. These tendencies can only be changed by uprooting the mental, emotional, and psychological conditions that cause their existence.

Any recidivist, especially one with three or four failures, obviously lacks a genuine understanding and acknowledgement of self-esteem. No man or woman that truly understands himself or herself would stay or be put in a position to be repeatedly incarcerated over a course of years or decades as an adult. There would have to be a profound and deep lack of self-understanding and self-determination. And this lack of self-understanding is perpetuated by a lack of self-acceptance – despite the fact that self-understanding is essential to our ability to change and grow.

When we do not accept something or someone, then we do not take the time to try to understand it, or him, or her. This applies likewise to ourselves. How we relate to ourselves operates no differently than the social laws of how we relate to others, except for one major exception: We can abuse, disrespect, and mistreat ourselves without ever having to worry about being confronted by others or accused by someone. This lack of worry unfortunately permits extensive self-abuse, especially in persons who have built a routine and constant negativity, even though such self-abuse is totally unproductive.

Recidivism arises from compulsive pathological tendencies toward economic (financial) and social achievement. Without question, these tendencies are generally or predominately dormant during phases of incarceration. It is no different than a smoker being denied access to cigarettes for a brief or even moderately extended period. Because he cannot smoke, he may assume that the inactive behavior frees him from nicotine addiction. He may, in fact, begin to think of himself as a non-smoker. However, once the denial of access is lifted, it isn't long before he is puffing again. Why? It's because he never truly made an internal commitment to not smoke; he simply attributed this goal or achievement to the effect of other forces or external conditions imposed on him.

Challenging the Pride System

Understand, first and foremost, that because of its defensive value the pride system is an autonomic system, and because of this it will resist just about any effort you make toward dismantling it to permit real growth. With each step along the way you must not only muster the strength to rebel against the pride system, but sustain faith in your ability to endure and conquer it. In challenging the pride system, you are actually embarking on a journey to war – a war within yourself. And unless you stand up and fight at every challenge, despite feelings of vulnerability, fear, helplessness, etc., the autonomous pride will defeat you.

For most people, the word unconscious is vague and undefined. It is a mysterious thing that they simply cannot grasp. For most of my life I heard the word and read about it in books, but couldn't really grasp the reality of it myself, even though I was profoundly driven by its content. I didn't really grasp the meaning of the unconscious until I began the psychoanalytic techniques of self-analysis – writing down childhood experiences as accurately and honestly as possible, allowing myself to feel what I felt from the experiences and even to feel what I had repressed from them: hurt, anger, resentment, rage. One has to bear in mind, through the pain of it all, that feelings can hurt but they can't kill. However, the compulsive behaviors that repressed feeling compel us to act out can kill, as well as destroy our lives in several other ways.

You have a choice. You can continue to suffer needlessly for who knows how much longer – years, decades, a lifetime – or you can suffer for an intense, brief period for a purpose. Either way there's going to be suffering – so why not get something out of it and end your compulsive criminality and cycle of imprisonment. You have to take a clear, honest, and level look at yourself and your life to acknowledge what basic needs you need to work at fulfilling. If you do not do this then the power of your repressed basic needs will compel you toward artificial or pathological expression of them.

The Path to Growth

1) Take an honest look at yourself and your life.

2) Acknowledge and feel the real impact of your personality deficiencies (basic need deprivations).

3) Identify how you need to work on emotions, thinking, education, and vocational skills.

4) Recognize how certain feelings or attitudes keep you down, or help you grow. Let go of self-destructive beliefs.

5) Consider how you yourself, alone or with the help of others, can change feelings that are contrary to your need to move forward.

6) Consider your current relationships. What influence or effect do certain people have on you? Who encourages you to be positive or negative?

7) Commit yourself to the work of freeing your mind from the compulsive criminal mentality.

8) Will yourself to be determined, but don't get the idea that will power is going to produce magical results. You must accept the reality of having to acknowledge the

obstructiveness of ideas and benefits that have long been detrimental to you. This means you have to face feelings instead of avoiding them. Be courageous. Overcome.

9) Be mindful of the fact that feelings can hurt, but they cannot kill. However, the unhealthy behaviors we adopt to repress hurtful feelings can result in many forms of self-destruction, even death.

10) Expect true transformation to be a long road; never forget that the road takes you to an invaluable destination.

CHAPTER 10

The Compulsive Criminal Mentality

This writing is not about the judicial and penal systems, but about the criminal mentality and a new approach to understanding and uprooting it. The term "compulsive criminal mentality" describes a class of offenders who are prone to recidivism because they are currently helpless against the emotional and psychological conditions that compel them to re-offend. These are conditions in the personality that they are not aware of consciously, because they've been repressed and psychologically evaded for years. That is, in simple terms, they are painful emotional needs that have been pushed out of awareness, and the feelings connected to them are thereby avoided.

This is about sharing what I know to help others better understand their condition. It isn't concerned with analyzing why one traumatized person becomes and offender while another one does not. It is not about justifying or excusing, as so many self-righteous cynics are quick to charge. It is about explaining why so many people are prone to re-offend, and offering insights that may help them break the cycle for good. It comes from the perspective that no matter when, where, or under what conditions one's criminality began, it is only from deep within that it can truly begin to end.

The Role Anxiety Plays

In the beginning we are all innocent children who have nothing to do with the crime, corruption, and violence in society. We are hardly even aware that these things exist. So how do people go from being innocent children to developing into repeat offenders, many tending to be violent, even murderous? Isn't it logical to think that people lost themselves somewhere along the way? Or do we continue to believe all the recidivism in society is simply caused by people freely choosing the wrong actions?

There's no doubt that thousands of people freely choose to commit crimes in America. But most of these people are so-called educated, well trained professionals, business people, etc. These are the people who freely choose to commit crimes. It isn't the people whose lives have been undermined before they even reach a level where freedom of choice is developed in the normal sense of the words. There is a human condition where, using the words of Karen Homey, M.D.: "Freedom of choice is negligible." This means that the capacity one has to make a free choice under certain conditions is virtually nonexistent.

What weakens the personality and character in this way, virtually robbing the individual of his or her free choice capacity is overwhelming anxiety. That is a fear that is generally irrational because it is out of proportion to the seriousness of the threat. This is what someone on the outside would see. But the person with the anxiety, and feeling seriously threatened, sees things differently. He or she sees things in crisis, with no alternative but to do what is most expedient to quell the anxiety.

If a person's achievement through criminal activity fortuitously becomes a consistent, expedient means of suppressing anxiety, then that person is likely to be a compulsive criminal, someone who, for all practical purposes, feels completely helpless against their criminal urges. Does this mean that they don't have a choice to not commit crimes? No. It means that because of their destructive personality condition, and the anxiety, they don't feel free to be patient and make the right or healthier choice.

Getting free from the anxiety as quickly as possible takes precedence over reason and rationale, law and justice, and the rights of others. The compulsive criminal when confronted with an anxiety crisis is about as free to choose not to relieve the anxiety with a criminal act, as an alcoholic in withdrawal is free to not choose his or her next drink. The power of free choice is negligible.

A lot of people may be thinking, what does anxiety have to do with committing crimes? Most people experience anxiety and still respect others. On the surface this appears completely true, but: (1) anxiety has a lot to do with repeat-offenders, and (2) we are not going to get anywhere by comparing law-abiders to non-law-abiders as a meaningless way to dispel excuses. This is about understanding and insight, and about outgrowing a personality and unhealthy social condition. There is a difference between an explanation and an excuse, but many people tend to blur the definitions.

Addictions and Compulsive Behaviors

The first time any person takes a drink, smokes a cigarette, or uses drugs is a free choice, isn't it? The answer is generally yes, but there are exceptions. The same applies to the first time a person commits a crime. But once the first engagement has taken place, a whole new relationship between thinking, feeling, psychology, and the behavior comes into being. Various personality conditions come into play, which determine whether the individual will smoke another cigarette, take another drink, use another shot or snort, or commit another crime. If the behavior relieves the individual of an emotional/psychological discomfort, or of stress or social anxiety, it is likely to be engaged in again. This is how addictions and compulsive behaviors develop.

Personalities in a weakened or underdeveloped condition interact with powerful stress- and anxiety-relieving substances, initiating addiction. Let us understand that the objective of crime, too, is the relief of emotional, psychological, social, or economic stresses and anxieties. Hence, criminality can become as addictive as cocaine, alcohol, etc. If you believe the alcoholic simply chooses to keep drinking, or the repeat offender simply chooses to keep committing crimes and revolving in and out of jails and prisons, then you are very mistaken. In both instances, the person needs help to develop emotional and psychological strength so that they can face conflicts and anxieties in a healthy way, and also exercise the Lr dormant capacity to freely choose what is in their best interest, as well as society's.

Psycho-Social Health and Happiness

What is it that causes such debilitated personality conditions and overwhelming anxiety, and obstructs the capacity for freedom of choice to the point that it becomes negligible? In general, the answer is unfulfilled basic psycho-social needs. In terms of psycho-social needs I am talking about the human soul and everything that has something to do with the core of ourselves being fulfilled and healthy.

As human beings, we are equipped with a natural set of healthy-operational need-demands, psycho-social as well as physical. Deprive the body of real vitamins and nutrients and a person will not be relieved of hunger or malnourishment, no matter how full the stomach is kept with vitamin- and nutrient-deficient foods. Deprive the psyche (soul) of feelings of self-worth, and no matter how much money and wealth a

77

person accumulates, he or she will still feel that they aren't valuable or worthy enough as a person.

Other basic psycho-social needs that cannot be artificially satisfied are self-confidence, love, affection, self-acceptance, and self-determination. In terms of psycho-social health and happiness, the degree to which we genuinely fulfill these basic needs has the greatest influence on our attitudes and experience in life. Their fulfillment or lack thereof has a lot to do with how we feel about ourselves at the core of our emotional being. To lose sight of this is to become alienated from our own nature. That's when artificial needs and false values become powerful, motivating forces in our lives.

The average repeat offender is suffering from the compulsive-criminal mentality. And this compulsiveness is rooted in his or her lack of basic-needs fulfillment.

So one may think, then why don't they fulfill their basic needs? The answer is that the needs, although always beckoning for genuine satisfaction, have been repressed in order for the person to evade the pain and suffering attached to their unfulfillment. The person has, in this sense, become alienated from his or her own core, and insatiable artificial needs have become the focus of their life pursuits. For example, a severe lack of self-esteem can force a person to repress feelings of worthlessness by seeking prestige. In this case, prestige becomes an artificial value that the person feels compelled to pursue. If always having fancy material possessions, clothes, plenty of money, etc., is the person's means of feeling recognized in the eyes of others, then the person could become a compulsive robber, drug dealer, etc., after being introduced to crime as a method.

As long as the individual has no self-esteem, he or she will need to repress feelings of worthlessness, and that need is what makes the artificial achievement of prestige through criminal activity compulsive. With little or no education and job training, the person is unlikely to gain employment that would provide sufficient and random access to money, hence, the answer to the question, why doesn't he or she work like everyone else?

Just as the alcoholic feels driven to drink in order to repress his or her feelings and anxieties, so does the compulsive criminal, or what's called the habitual offender. The offender feels that he or she must avoid his or her feelings of worthlessness and self-hate at all costs, just as the alcoholic avoids the pain. At the same time, he or she must avoid the feeling of being perceived by others as worthless, therefore rejectable and meaningless. And the fear of being consciously confronted with all these self-belittling feelings is literally the fear of facing a tortuous anxiety. It is an anxiety hidden from the outside world, but none the less real. But even more tragic is the fact that the root causes of the offender's anxiety and compulsiveness are as out of reach from his conscious perception as they are from anyone else's. It is no wonder, then, that he or she can spend a whole lifetime repeating offenses and incarcerations, haunted by the mystery of why they haven't changed, and seemingly cannot for the life of themselves.

If you are one of those people sitting in a prison cell right now, after having already served two, three, or however many other terms of incarceration as a juvenile and/or adult, and you are still castigating yourself under the causative guise of 'simply' having made another mistake or bad decision, what are you going to say next time? Get it in your head that you aren't so stupid that you'd keep coming back over and over again if you were really free to choose otherwise. Admit that you have been enslaved by the condition of compulsive criminality, then begin the long, hard process of uprooting that condition within yourself. There are lots of people who've earned college degrees, been religious devotees, written a book, taught advance mathematics while in prison, who have gone home but returned for new offenses. It isn't always what you do with yourself, but what you undo within yourself that uproots the condition of the compulsive criminal mentality.

CHAPTER 11

Neurotic Pride and Self-Confidence

There are two types of pride that may operate in the human mind. One is the healthy pride, which always expresses itself as a pride in something particular, as Karen Homey taught in her Understanding: "Pride is always pride in something."

This expression is healthy pride. For example, I can have pride in my accomplishments. I can be proud of my moral integrity, proud of my academic achievements, etc.

It is always a concrete pride.

On the other hand, there is neurotic pride, and it is an unhealthy and unproductive phenomenon operating in the mind. Neurotic pride is a compensatory development in direct correspondence to deficiencies of success and fulfillment in one's natural evolution. It is not a realistic pride in anything particular, but a "Pride for the sake of pride itself" In this sense, neurotic pride is an inflated opinion of oneself that operates as a life vest to keep one from drowning in self-hate and self-contempt. On the surface, however, this type of pride appears to be something that it is not: it masquerades as self-confidence.

The Lack of Self-Confidence

Norney pointed out in Neurosis and Human Growth that "Self-confidence is based on one's real accomplishments. Neurotic pride, in imaginary achievements." An individual may, for example, experience pride in the accomplishments of his ancestors as though he were/is actually a part of those accomplishments, as though he did some of the work himself. Imagine how desperate a person must be to find something admirable about himself if he resorts to such a measure. But you must understand that this measure is partly unconscious in it operation.

You see, he is not always aware of his lack of self-confidence because the neurotic pride protects him from that awareness.

There are many who have achieved little, if anything, in life; imagine that person: high school dropout, no vocational skills, no measurable development of talent, a succession of failed relationships, a string of job losses, whether quitting, not meeting the grade, or being fired, and add to this a list of criminal convictions and sentences from which nothing meaningful, in the sense of genuine change, has occurred. Where does this person point, to find the personal successes that would undergird the existence of real self-confidence? Self-confidence is based on one's accomplishments, so where are his accomplishments? If he is viewed as a failure at everything in life, and unconsciously views himself as an utter failure, then he has no confidence, not in the real, legitimate sense, at least. In this condition, maybe even as early as his late childhood, he has two options: (1) Learn to accomplish what is necessary to build his self-confidence, or (2) unwittingly spiral into the abyss of hopelessness, and begin to construct an artificial pride system to repress the tortuous feelings of self-hate and the utter lack of genuine confidence in oneself.

Develop Real Confidence

Real confidence strengthens the character and allows one to face life's challenges with determination and personal faith. Pride is a weakness when it is pride for pride's sake. It buckles under the real pressures of life and cannot withstand much frustration. If fact, neurotic pride tends to influence one to withdraw from ever facing basic life challenges, if they threaten one's sense of equality or supremacy.

From what we see above, it is absolutely necessary that real confidence be developed and the grip of neurotic pride be substantially weakened if recidivism is to be avoided and the propensities toward it overcome. Any prior recidivist should not take this self-evaluation and the related responsibility for granted; the more failures, then the more pressing the need. One has to understand and remain aware that the need for neurotic pride arise from desperate internal conditions, so that challenging one's pride is not going to be a smooth and easy contest.

What all recidivists need to understand is that 'pride', for many people, is all that they have to make them feel worthy of existing in this world. So, any challenge to one's pride can set some very uncomfortable and distressing emotions into operation. Boldly facing these uncomfortable and distressing emotions is the first step to overcoming them. You must overcome, because as long as you are in the grip of neurotic pride, instead of in the embrace of constructive and genuine self-confidence, you will be unable to withstand true challenges in the world and persevere in facing many of life's most basic responsibilities; at least, not for long.

False Pride

Don't leave yourself exposed to the weaknesses and vulnerabilities of a false pride mentality. And, do not remain a victim of the illusion often created and maintained by false

83

pride, the illusion that confidence falls out of the sky. Self-confidence is the product of one's accomplishments, not one's imagination or failures.

The idea of having pride in ourselves because of what others before us have accomplished is an absurdity under the laws of cause and effect. But there are people who actually think this way. It is like believing you can win a gold boxing medal because the new champ looks like you, and the similar looks alone give you confidence in yourself. This type of thinking is symptomatic of some deep underlying problem in one's relationship with self, and one's understanding of the difference between pride and self-confidence. You are going to have to face the truth about yourself in order to know your strengths and weaknesses.

If you cannot become aware of and accept the truth, then you undermine your ability to change your reality, no matter how unfortunate and self-defeating that reality may be. Recidivism is not a problem you simply outgrow or overcome by chance. It has to be confronted and overcome as a matter of conscious and self-determined choice. Other can offer you information and insight, but it is up to you to gain understanding and wisdom.

The Lack of Confidence

Anytime a person lacks basic confidence, he or she falls short of making efforts to achieve the goals that are naturally basic in general society; sometimes these goals may be as basic as high school graduation, a GED, and some type of direction towards vocational training skills. But even with these achievements, recidivism still looms large over the lives of hundreds of thousands. Why? It is because the wages earned by an individual with only a little education or vocational training do not satisfy the material and social desires of a person who is operating with shortages in basic psycho-social need fulfillments.

This person's emotional, psychological, and spiritual hungers tend to produce excessive demands upon himself or herself, and others. Lack of confidence deters a great deal of initiative, effort, and striving toward goals in society. To begin with, confidence is based on one's successful achievement of other previous goals, dreams, etc. We build confidence from one successful endeavor to another. The more we achieve, the more capable we become of having confidence to achieve even greater things. The less we achieve, even in small ways, the less confident we are in our abilities. This leads many to become vulnerable to seeking economic and social achievement through illegal methods, which are much more expedient and much less time-consuming. Here again, the lack of fulfillment of basic needs results in the development of pathology and excessive-need feelings.

The Lack of Self-Love

Our relationship with ourselves is the primary relationship. If we do not love ourselves, then it is because we do not accept ourselves enough. It follows then, that too little or no self-acceptance sets into operation at least two types of pathology by which we artificially compensate. (1) Through the power of our imaginative faculties, we begin to create an artificial self, or an idealized self. (2) We place excessive value on gaining the acceptance of others. Sometimes this reaches the extreme degree of a need for constant confirmation of being acceptable.

How does this tie into recidivism? Being in the grip of a need for self-esteem drives many under-educated and under-skilled people to pursue material wealth and financial power beyond their legitimate capabilities to earn. The lack of self-

esteem and the low self-acceptance are mitigated in their effect (pain, suffering, torment) by the spurious achievement of social esteem. And the social esteem becomes such a desperate need that the individual may have no perception whatsoever of so-called friends as merely associates who have no true interest in him or
her other than what they can gain, even if that gain for themselves is no more than prestige for themselves (likely "friends" being probably also deficit in basic-needs fulfillment).

Since artificial needs can never be fulfilled to the point of satisfying the hunger of genuinely basic needs, they operate as insatiable forces of hunger in the mind. They will compel a person beyond all reason and rationale until he or she is rid of them - or the insatiable needs have rid the person (in the case of the recidivist), of his or her freedom. And, once released from prison, the cycle begins again.

PSEUDO-SOLUTIONS

A lot of things that work to change the thinking and behavior of of other offenders don't work for the compulsive offender. They are therefore pseudo-solutions to his problems, even though he pursues them with feelings of sincerity, whether vocations, religion, G.E.D., even college. While these achievements may change the lives of some offenders who are not compulsive in their criminality, the compulsive offender must achieve something much greater. He must achieve the inner power of free choice and self-determination, both of which are sadly lacking in his character. The ordinary rehabilitation pseudo-solution won't provide those; on the streets, criminal acts won't either – they are another kind of pseudo-solution.

A pseudo-solution is a solution (such as a criminal act) that appears to be the solution to a problem but eventually proves not to be. For the compulsive repeat offender, the scenario is very real he commits criminal acts over and over again because the objective of the crimes operates as a pseudo-solution.

Almost everything in this condition of compulsive criminality exists as part of a self-perpetuating, vicious cycle that actually overwhelms the individual himself. He is a slave to the unconscious forces that drive him, as well as to the false pride that he mistakenly thinks can free him from those forces of enslavement, vulnerability, and self-hate.

For example, consider the individual who is void or deficient in all the psycho-social necessities. A tormenting lack of self-worth looms in the forefront of his subconscious assailants. Within the context of society's cultural values, money becomes the pseudo-solution (compensation) for his lack of feelings of self-worth. Without money he fears that he will be perceived by others as he unconsciously perceives himself – as meaningless and worthless. His means of frequently possessing money is through crime; hence, his criminality becomes compulsive because he is driven to maintain the artificial structure of self-worth and prestige that he has built around money.

The Pride System

In the theory of advanced psychoanalysis, the pride system consists of the sum total of excuses, illusions, denials, rationalizations, and unconscious defense mechanisms employed to protect oneself from the psychological torment of self-hate and all that it involves. The pride system is also a protector of the idealized self, which is itself a desperate counter to self-hatred. The difference between neurotic pride and healthy pride is that neurotic pride is not based on substantial achievements or qualities within oneself; it is based on the all-consuming need to glorify oneself, to raise oneself above one's real condition and status, not by actual work and achievement, but by imagination.

As long as the pride system operates as the mainstay of one's emotional and psychological sense of stability and confidence, one will never be able to put forth realistic efforts, because one will be oblivious to one's own real needs in terms of a conscious acceptance. What this means is that in order to meet your real needs you must begin to see yourself realistically, and that means decreasing your degree of, and dependence on, neurotic pride. A firmly entrenched pride system generally functions independently of your conscious will; in fact, it can compel you to act and react in many ways that aren't in your best interest, and then you condemn and criticize yourself for having done so. This, in itself, becomes a self-depreciating cycle.

As you work to weaken the pride system, you must simultaneously decrease the condition of self-hate, otherwise the pride system will simply switch from one compulsive expression to another. Just as some people imagine themselves to be more than they are, others imagine themselves to be less. In general, both over-exaggerated conditions exist in the same person. One has to struggle to get back to middle ground (so to speak) where one is not unrealistically elevated or submerged, but standing face to face with the reality of his or her life.

Since neurotic pride is a pseudo-solution to the absence of self-confidence from the character structure, you need to be careful about the possible illusion of having self-confidence. False confidence always expresses itself as anxiety and frustration when put to the test because it is an illusion created within the pride system. Real confidence rests on a solid foundation of effort and achievement, thereby giving one the belief that future success is possible.

PART THREE:

The Change Process

When it comes to learning about the change process, time and constancy are the key ingredients. As you stick with it, over days, weeks, and months, certain elements of what you learn become hardwired. Slowly, change becomes internalized, part of your nervous system. The difference is not simply a matter of determination, but of trust and faith. By trusting the process, you will allow natural learning to happen, and everything else will fall into place.

CHAPTER 12

Change is Possible

It takes a while before people realize change is possible. At first, most people do not believe or understand they have a problem. But gradually people get tired of their way of life, and become more open-minded to the idea of change. Then they become willing to explore the possibility of change more seriously.

Although change is possible, change is not initially easy, because change represents adapting to a different way of thinking and living. We get so used to living a certain way, it makes the process of change hard because our destructive lifestyles and the power of addiction is still within us and around us.

It is important to remember that change is not an overnight process. Change in character and behavior comes gradually as we become open to accepting a different way of life.

Considering Change

This is an opportunity for you to consider the path of your future. The decision to change or not is yours. This chapter can help you apply proven strategies of positive life change no matter where you are today. By considering positive changes, you will have the chance to work toward a responsible life full of rewards and freedoms.

The key to changing is to first recognize that all change is self-change. Authority figures or the legal system can pressure you to get started, but successful life change ultimately comes down to you and the choices you make. Even if you already started down the path of positive change, working through this chapter will increase the chance that you'll stick to your path, and that your changes will stick to you.

Imagine where you want to be and who you want to see in the mirror five or ten years from now. What do you need to work on to become that person? What changes do you need to make in yourself? If your behaviors and your values don't match, it can be a sign that it is time to make a change.

The Process of Change

The process of change begins by your being honest about your past behavior and actions, especially surrounding your criminality. Many are unable to understand why they did what they did. Some carry guilt and shame; others glorify what they did; while others simply don't want to think or talk about it.

No one is born a criminal; criminality is a learned behavior and series of habits. Think back to your first time doing something illegal – can you see how as you got older the pattern of criminality continued to escalate until it got out of control.

Here are some questions about change:
  1) Do you believe it is important to understand your past?
  2) When you made bad decisions, did you make them alone or were you influenced by others?

91

3) Do you understand how your criminal behavior continued to get worse?

4) Do you still indulge in criminal activities today?

5) Why is it important for you to change your life and criminal ways?

Breaking old habits and replacing them with new habits is an unfamiliar process. The key for this to work is to actually be willing to change. You have to be willing to let go of negative thoughts, words, and actions that could possibly cause problems for yourself and others. Although it will be hard at first, your willingness to let go is proof that you are sincere in your efforts to change your ways and lifestyle.

Be Honest About Your Change

It is very important to be honest with yourself about your change process. If you cannot be honest with yourself, your recovery will be at a standstill. When you look back on your past, you can clearly see how your lack of honesty affected your character through behaviors and actions. Today, with the process of change offered, you can open up and begin to be more honest about what needs your focus and attention.

Honesty opens doors to repairing broken relationships while promoting healthier ones. Honesty will put personal responsibility back in order. Once you can be accountable for yourself through honest self-examination, change becomes more meaningful.

Here are some questions about honesty:

1) How honest are you to yourself concerning your need to change?

2) Do you have difficulty being honest with yourself? If so, why?

3) What reasons to you use to make excuses for not being honest?

4) Can you think of ways honesty has helped you improve a relationship?

5) How does honesty improve your change process?

Feelings of Change

Making changes to habits often comes with uncomfortable feelings. At some point, the way you think and behave becomes a habit. People who are angry and abusive may have practiced faulty thinking for so long that it has become a habit for them. If that's true for you, remember that you control your thoughts and behavior. You can change negative habits and adopt positive behavior. This involves changing the way you think. It doesn't matter how long you've practiced faulty thinking habits, you can still change.

Whenever you try to change a habit, you will go through a period in which your thoughts and feelings do not match. You are out of your comfort zone, and it feels like an alarm has been set off in your brain. So as you work to develop new ways of thinking, it's important to learn how to successfully handle the uncomfortable feeling that occurs when you try to change a habit. Positive life changes, including changing your thinking patterns, will feel uncomfortable at first.

The key is to be able to deal with the uncomfortable feeling long enough to overcome the old habit. Strategies for Changing

Some things you can do are especially effective in your change process. The: following five strategies will help you as you work to make the changes you want.

1) Be A Role Model:
Your behavior sets an example for others. Think about becoming a role model by managing your anger,

Controlling your substance abuse, and stopping your illegal activity. Understand the difference between the

Negative influence of unhealthy behaviors and the positive impact of healthy behaviors on the people around you.

2) Reflect Your Values:

Changing your behavior for the better can improve the way you feel about yourself. Think about what you value in life. Does your behavior reflect your values? For example, some people see themselves as supportive partners, spouses, or parents, but their abusive behavior doesn't match.

3) Commit To Change:

If you believe you can change and are willing to take action, make a commitment to do so. Share your plan to change with others, so you are more likely to get support and be successful with your commitment. Saying it out loud can be powerful.

4) Turn Negatives Into Positives:

Replace negative thoughts and behaviors with positive ones. You can do this by taking a walk to cool down when you become angry instead of being abusive to others. You might also choose to talk to someone who can help you see the situation differently.

5) Adjust Your Environment:

Adjusting your environment may help you make a healthy behavior change. For example, if using drugs or alcohol led to violence for you in the past, do not keep it in your home. Keep it out of your environment.

Make the Decision to Change

You cannot change anything unless you make a personal decision to do so. What you fail to change you can be certain will be repeated over and over again. If you want to change, you have to start making changes in yourself, then your behavior will naturally follow.

You have the ability to make decisions between good/right or bad/wrong. The first brings peace and harmony while the opposite brings pain and destruction.

In the past you chose to do bad/wrong, but you can choose to improve your choices and decisions. Then you will begin doing what is right/good for yourself – as you do, those positive choices will naturally affect those around you.

It will be hard doing good when you're so used to doing wrong. Your ego will deceive you and try to convince you that you are weak to even try to do good. But you are actually learning it is weak to do wrong, taking the easy way out.

As you open the door to change, you'll demonstrate courage and confidence instead of fear and shame. You may not be perfect, but you're also not incapable of bettering yourself.

Committing to Change

So far in this chapter you have explored the impact of your behaviors and prepared yourself to commit to making changes. Making a commitment to change is a turning point in your life. It is a clear shift, away from living in the past to having a vision of the future you want for yourself. But, the idea of making a commitment to change is sometimes hard to grasp.

Consider your commitment to change as part of your foundation for your future. Just like with buildings, a life with a weak foundation is at a higher risk of collapsing than one with a strong foundation. The foundation supports the entire structure. One way to help you build a sturdy foundation for your commitment to change is to constantly imagine yourself living a responsible life; think about the rewards that would come over time.

Another way to help you build a sturdier foundation for your commitment to change is to create a support network. Relying on the support of other people in your life can help you make positive changes. These people will provide the safety net that you will depend on as you take steps toward responsible living.

As you build your support network, consider the following four categories:
- Supportive family members
- Responsible friends
- Role models
- Professional help.

The entire next chapter is about this important topic.

Setting Change Goals

Setting goals is a powerful tool in making positive life changes. Goals help give you direction; short-term and long-term goals let you know where you are and where you want to go. Short-term goals are the action steps along the way toward your long-term goals. As time goes by, you'll review and revise your goals to be sure you are on the right path.

Set goals that are realistic: you must have the physical capabilities, knowledge, skills, motivation, and resources to be successful at achieving your goals. If you feel that your goal is not realistic, step back and aim for a more reasonable target. You want your goals to move you toward a more responsible lifestyle, you want them to be in the best interest of you, the people you care about, and society as a whole.

To accomplish your goals and maintain your success, your goals will need to hold value for you. Meaningful goals are driven by the desire to make changes for yourself that start on the inside and become visible to others as a result of your behaviors.

GET OUT, STAY OUT

CHAPTER 13

Your Support Networks

Knowing that change is possible and being committed to the process of change are an excellent start on your journey to GETTING OUT. Moving forward, your chances of success will be hugely improved if you surround yourself with a strong support network to provide the necessary and critical help you need to make those life changes you've committed to. As you build your support network, you will seek out people who will be able to provide you with honest and objective feedback, and who will stick with you through the whole program.

You will most likely find these people among these groups:

- Members of your family and extended family;
- Friends, coworkers, and other healthy peers;
- Teachers, mentors, or role models; and
- Professional helpers (counselor, therapist, clergy).

Support: Two Kinds, Two Motives

The support you need in prison isn't the same as you will need when you get out, so you will actually have two support networks. There will be overlap, of course, especially of your closest outside supporters, likely your family.

While you're still in prison, your support network and the use you make of it should be, will be, all about GETTING OUT. It will include, of course, your most loyal family and friends outside, but it should include other persons, inside and out, and also the impersonal help you get from attending formal self-help groups.

When you get out of prison, your support network and the use you make of it should be, will be, all about STAYING OUT. It will include those same loyal family and friends, and others that you will recruit (hopefully before you leave prison) and a few that the process (or luck, or fate, or blessing) will bring to you.

(Don't even think about including old "friends" who are still doing the things that got you into orison in the first place or that contributed to your fall. Even if you're not one of those with a criminal-compulsive nature (see Chapter 10) there's no reason to put yourself in the midst of temptation and several reasons not to for example, your parole officer.)

Never forget that you yourself are a critical member of your own support network. Your assignment is harder than any other: you must manage without stepping on toes, and be boss without being demanding. Further, you have to actually make-the effort that's being supported - your rehabilitation. It's your job to supply the intangibles that are power for the work and grease for the axle - courtesy, trust tons and tons of gratitude and love, and faith.

Build Your Support Network

You might be able to accomplish all you intend by yourself, but the best way to help yourself with your commitment to change is to build a support network. Relying on the support of other people in your life will help you in your quest for positive change. In the same way that one group of people once influenced you to irresponsible behaviors, another group will now support your efforts to make responsible changes.

You will put people into your support network to provide the safety net that you'll depend on as you steps toward responsible living, and maintain your achievements both before and after release. You will be a lot more confident in your efforts with the knowledge that there are others who want to see you succeed. The four best options for building your support network are

1) Supportive family members.

This group includes those members of your family who will support you by holding you accountable for your choices and behaviors. Do not add family members to your support network who encourage or defend your irresponsible behaviors. Pick those people who are supportive of your positive changes, and who will provide the direct and honest feedback that is essential to keep you from sliding into thought errors and problem behaviors.

Yes, these are the same people you hope will send you stamps, money, and packages; that's fine. Just remember that these things shouldn't be your primary expectation of your supporters. Sure, they help keep you comfortable, but in fact you probably shouldn't permit yourself to be too comfortable in prison – the less you like it, the more likely you are to avoid whatever would send you back to prison.

2) Responsible friends.

Such special friends as you choose will support you pretty much as if they were family; you'll expect them to hold you accountable, and to set an example for you. Like family, friends can also provide financial support, but that's never a primary purpose.

A very few in this category, before you leave prison, might be other prisoners, or even prison staff. More is said about this further down.

3) Role models.

Role models include those people who show by example a positive, responsible lifestyle. These are the people who talk the talk and walk the walk. They may be people who have overcome big life challenges and now want to help others. Or, they may simply be people you know who have dealt with hard times while remaining humble, honest, responsible, and willing. They may even be people you've never met, perhaps a great-grandfather you've heard about from your family, or some celebrity who shows a true caring for his or her responsibility to society.

By the way, don't be disappointed if one of your role models messes up. Nobody is perfect – just forgive and move on, but don't copy the failure. If the role model is a friend or family member, it's time for you to be part of his or her "support network". Show compassion, give good, honest counsel, and continue to set a good example: you be the role model.

4) Professional help.

Professional help includes people with special skills and knowledge who can support your positive behaviors. To get the most from professionals that you recruit to help you, you need to be honest. Resist keeping secrets about issues or problems. Remember, if you don't ask for help, you won't receive it. Professional help includes therapists or counselors, counseling groups, members of the clergy, vocational or educational counselors. In addition to their professional help, they can offer advice about employment or education opportunities, or other community resources.

The "Characters" In Your Support Network

Generally speaking, both in prison and after release, your support network must contain people who serve you in these roles: you need a counselor/advisor, a confidant, a communicator/organizer, a legal aide, a research assistant, a material supplier, a financial backer, and a Dutch-Uncle/enforcer. If you have only a few family members helping, each will likely fill more than one of these roles; this is typical, because your support network shouldn't be too big. Likely, right now, some of these roles are unfilled.

Probably, no role is more important than any other, but all are needed at some time or other – a few only occasionally, some constantly. Some you may fill yourself, like legal aid or research assistant, or even financial backer if you have a plum job in or out of prison. Most of the role 'titles' are adequate descriptions of what they'll do, but you may be wondering about that last one.

Traditionally, a "Dutch Uncle" is someone who will tell it like it is, without holding back, without pulling punches. We're not talking here about having a personal full-time critic, but you will need some special person, both inside and outside, that you trust and respect, that you assign to watch you for signs of falling off your change path, to tell you so, and to help you back (the "enforcer" part). Sure, you will maybe chafe a little at such a "leash", but it's better than needing an intervention from your family, or worse, from police.

Express Your Goals

Before putting people into your support network, express your goals to them. Have a clear plan about how you will ask for their support; you have to explain what sorts of help you need from them, how it will help you achieve your goals, and what your commitments are that merit the support. Your prospective members aren't accepted just because they show up for a visit, or send a package (though those are signs of their commitment); you'll want them to understand your goals and agree to help fulfill some of the roles listed above. Tell each one of your decision to build a support network of chosen people; tell them that this is a priority for you; be clear that you need their help to be successful. You'll be expressing your goals with every member of your support network, and with others who will help you achieve your goals.

Part of the reason to share your goals and plans is to give everyone the big picture and let them know how their contribution fits; but, importantly, it's a fact that when you share your goals with others, it increases your own commitment to those goals.

Ask For Help

When you've developed your support network and expressed your goals for change, you will be able to tap into your support network at need. They will help you succeed in your efforts to change. Even though you are the only person who can change your behaviors, you don't have to do it alone. That's good news – you now have people you know are committed to helping you. You can get incentive when your motivation is running low; you can get encouragement when you are distracted or facing temptations. Your support network will help you stick to your plan and work toward your goals. But they won't know you need help if you don't ask.

As you recruited these people, you explained the kinds of situations you might encounter, and together you worked out what sort of help might be needed (you did share your plan, right?). So when you need help, you must ASK; they are ready, prepared, and committed. Keep your network informed of of your progress (your 'communicator" might help with this); give thanks profusely for help, both the kind that's constant, and the kind you call for when there's problems. And, keep making the effort at change and rehabilitation which is, at heart, the reason for the network in the first place. Your effort and progress is a big part of the payback you give that keeps everybody happy for you. Maintaining that effort, that momentum, will not be easy; it will require your dedication and constant effort. But think – what else do you have to do in prison or that's more important than working to get out of prison. Nothing. Give it your all.

Keep a written record – a journal or diary – to help you keep track of your progress, your thoughts, what you say to yourself, how you feel, and what things occasionally interfere with or help your plan. Reviewing it will give you incentive to carry on, with the help you've earned from your support network.

Support While in Prison

While you are working to GET OUT, a solid support network and family backing are essential to your preparations for the Board and to getting a parole date. Your support network will be mostly your family and friends, but a few roles may be filled with people you meet in prison; choosing these inmate-helpers requires much care and probably a long time before settling on choices.

Certainly, always cultivate friendly relations with other inmates, but keep your close circle very small – just a few others who are also committed to change. They may be participants in your groups, or even leaders there. They may be fellow students, or some few that you meet through your church. Reject those who disappoint; avoid anyone who bullies, mocks, or gossips about others; avoid those who bait officers. Avoid any who show the least cruelty or disrespect. And remember, others are evaluating you as possible help – don't disappoint them.

Remember the special nature of the confidant and Dutch-Uncle roles; if an inmate will fill one of these roles, he or she must be a very special person indeed.

Your outside people are always most important to you. You need their lava and their support, both "moral, and financial; you need their visits and their shared help with planning; you need their contributions to your program of change. They must be supportive, persistent, and resourceful. Remember always that they are sacrificing to provide the important help you can't get anywhere else – as a consequence, referring to those tons and tons of gratitude and love mentioned earlier, you must give back what you get: love, respect, forgiveness; you can't repay exactly "in kind', but you can give your helpers satisfaction in knowing that you continue to do what you promised them and yourself: constant progress with never a snide comment or angry word, and as few "situations" as possible. Every visit must be clean; every letter must be respectful; every phone call must be aware that there are others listening and maybe there's a recording. Such "rules" are not because C/0's might be paying attention, but because such courtesy is the proper way to treat your own people.

Your outside supporters have access that you don't – to help you prepare for the Board, they can do these things that you can't, all of which can greatly increase your chances of parole, by demonstrating to the Board that you are not only "changed", but extremely well prepared, as well:

1) Your family and friends outside should provide letter of support. They are vital (see Chapter 3). Your direct support network can also work to get support letters from others who knew you favorably, like former employers. It is crucial that these letters be updated for each hearing, and that they be original signed documents.

2) Your support network members are your eyes, ears, and legs on the outside; they can find you job offers, investigate their quality; they can find you the locations of self-help

rehabilitative groups (AA/NA), maybe even get you enrolled, or introduced to sponsors, and meeting schedules and locations. These kinds of details and progress can be very effectively made part of the written parole plan you provide to the Board.

3) We've already discussed not only how reading self-help books can help you to make the changes you need, but also how writing reports on such books can contribute to the Board's positive opinion of your personal self-help efforts. Your people outside can help find and provide books on self-help, books specifically for book reports, and correspondence education courses. Let them know you can ep only so many books, but don't discourage them; just let them know when you've finished with each book so they can send another. Donate your books to the library, ask for receipts: this will not only gain you favorable points in your file, but will also provide a record of the books that pass through your self-help program.

4) The more detail you can include in your parole plan to the Board, and the more steps in it already completed, the better. Your outside support can help you fill in the details for your short- or long-term parole plans, and prepare the way so you can accomplish quickly what you'll need to do on release. Among these are problems like getting a driver's license, getting a social security number (for both of these you might need a copy of your birth certificate). They may be able to get letters showing real job offers. They can investigate issues with transportation and living arrangements, perhaps agreeing to provide housing for a certain time while you earn money for your own place.

5) They can investigate and perhaps even help you enroll or apply for benefits you may be entitled to on release. These can include Veteran's benefits, Social Security benefits, and so on. There is more material on possible benefits in Part Five. Applying for some of these benefits may require

documentation that your supporters can secure for you, saving you time and avoiding possible exposure or loss in the prison mail system.

6) One way they can help is interesting and potentially useful-- your outside supporters can check with the Controllers' unclaimed funds website. A surprising number of inmates have money owed to them that's being held for them by the Controller's unclaimed funds division. While these funds can't be sent to you in prison, they can be accessed once you are released; they can often be several hundred dollars. (These funds are from unclaimed checks, wages, bank accounts, insurance settlements, and the like, that you may have been owed but not collected prior to incarceration.)

7) It's likely that your supporters regularly, or at least occasionally, send you money for canteen, or send you packages. If you ask, they might be willing to send you a little less money, or buy a cheaper package, and put the difference into a savings account that would be yours on release. A dollar so saved would become about $1.55 after 15 years at 3%. Such a saving plan could provide a very nice nest egg when you leave prison.

Support When You Leave Prison

When you are working to STAY OUT, a solid network and family support are essential to ease you back into society, to help you put your parole plan into action, to get you through problems that threaten to derail you, to provide promised resources the Board counted on, to help and encourage you to maintain the progress you made in prison, and to continue making progress now that you're out. You should never consider yourself finished.

Remember that though these people love you very much, they are not going to hover around you attending to every need and problem. First of all, you are a proper man or woman in your own right, and, as we've said elsewhere, you are responsible for yourself. Secondly, part of the idea is that you have to ask. Don't hesitate, or be embarrassed that you need help – remember, they WANT to help. They agreed to help. Just don't forget to perform: effort, improvement, and gratitude.

There are lots of very specific things that your support network can do for you. Exactly what happens will vary from case to case. Here are some suggestions:

1) You'll know your release date 45 to 60 days beforehand; when it's firmed up, your supporters can send you parole clothes; they can be sure they know where your parole officer wants you to report, and when. They can arrange to pick you up from the prison or bus stop, and take you to where you'll spend your first night; they can take you to the parole office on time, same day or next.

2) They may want to plan a family "reunion" to welcome you back. That's fine; you should probably ask them to not do that on the first day out - you will probably have been up since 3AM, and maybe travelled hundreds of miles by bus or car. You'll feel more like attending a reunion after you've had a couple of days to settle in. The same thing goes for whatever good first-food you've decided you want after you get out.

3) They can take you shopping; they can make sure you get to places you need to be maybe even to some job interviews. Just put your plan into action, ask for the help you need when you need it, and things will work out; if they don't, ask for help.

Things won't be the same; some things will seem scary; some things will just be strange, or even marvelous. As time goes by, you will become more and more used to being on your own, and things will be better and better. Remember the five-year rule. Just keep plugging.

Seek Support

When you are no longer incarcerated, you have both opportunity and responsibility to find support from sources other than your support network. There are groups, services, and other resources available to support you. Look around for any support groups or self-help meetings, or any places that seem to support people who are working to change their lives, too. Even if you simply watch others in these places at first, you will see the kind of support that is available if you choose to join in the activities. In seeking support, consider these: Attending religious services; Enrolling in a class that focuses on learning a skill; and Joining a recreation group or organized support group that is made up of helpful people with worthwhile programs.

Look at all your options to help you decide what you're best choices are; seek the advice of your support network in this. Choose the options you believe are the best fit for you and your situation.

Always keep your support network informed of what you are doing to continue your progress toward your long-term goals. Letting them know that you - ARE progressing, and how, is part of the way you thank them for their help.

Unbuilding Your Support Network

As your life becomes more and more stable after release, your need for help from others will decrease; you'll need less help, perhaps none, other than continued association and love. But you'll never tell anyone, "Hey, I don't need you anymore!" That would seem to be a put-down. You must signal your reduced need with praise and thanks: "Thanks for helping me back then; I'm doing a lot better now. I couldn't have done it without you; thanks so much."

This kind of treatment will make a great mutual trust and respect – your family and friends will be less burdened, and they'll know that if you later ask for something, you really, really need it.

The One Supporter You Should Seek First and Keep Forever

If you have the slightest spark of faith in a divine being, God, you will do very well to cultivate that faith, and accept Him as a member of your support network, from the very beginning.

According to most faiths, He wants to help you; it's the very definition of grace. As your faith grows, you'll discover that He's always helped you already, as bad as things may have seemed. Such faith, as much or more than any other support, can carry you through tough times in prison and beyond, and move you away from situations (even those beyond your control) that might pull you off your plans. Remember, when things are worrisome, He's the only supporter you can always talk to immediately; He will always listen and answer, somehow – you may not see it, but His answer will always be what's best for you.

CHAPTER 14

Victim Awareness

You are who you are today because of the choices you made throughout your life concerning how you responded to others and what you did; how you were raised also affected who you are today because every bit of your history influenced your choices. There was a time when you made a choice to practice irresponsible and illegal behaviors.

You may not have realized it at the time, but your criminal behavior created a ripple effect. It affected your immediate victims directly; then, through the ripple effect, it affected their families, your family, you, and ultimately many more. Others in society became more fearful, lost time or sleep because of you. Perhaps a youth saw some excitement or enticement in the notoriety and attention you received and decided to copy you, and so your crime rippled out to a second set of victims. All the people – officials, associates of the victims, bystanders – who had to deal with any part of the situation you created were affected by the need to spend personal capital as your ripple passed them; they, too, are your victims.

The Board will expect you to know and understand all this and more; they will also expect you to demonstrate your understanding by showing "victim awareness".

In order to understand victim awareness, and the closely related ideas of remorse, amends, restitution, and healing, you must first: review the criminal offense that brought you to prison, and develop some shame and sadness for the harm it did to all your victims; examine the ripple effect that resulted from your behavior, and extend your understanding to the true scope of the harm you've done; learn how to begin to make amends to the people you've harmed; if you've truly considered the ripple effect, your heart should be broken, and you'll have a deep, true desire to make things right again; and create a personal plan that includes taking responsibility for your behavior; in other words, you will actually do things that could reduce the burden you placed on the expanding, rippling circle that reached so many victims.

Your Committing Offense

Your journey to a responsible life requires a clear understanding of your committing offense and the effects it had on many more people than you probably thought. True responsibility comes when you take ownership of the damaging effects of your criminal behavior, understand the nature and magnitude of all the harm you caused, make amends as possible to those you have harmed, and make a commitment to a positive, crime-free lifestyle, such commitment including the effort required to achieve that lifestyle.

The task of understanding your committing offense will take time and effort. You may need to complete several versions of your committing-offense story as your honesty with yourself increases and you gain awareness of the impact you made; in this way you will build a better understanding of victim awareness. Up until now, you may have taken the easy path and made all the excuses you could to avoid responsibility; you may be inclined to continue to make such excuses. That won't help your victims, and it won't help you. The Board requires the understanding outlined in this chapter; without it, you probably won't get out as you wish. Besides, did you not make a commitment to change as you read the earlier chapters? Making excuses is inconsistent with that commitment; lying to yourself about your committing offense is inconsistent with that commitment. You must move forward with empathy and true understanding of how you impacted the lives of your victims, and you must add activities to your new lifestyle that will, as mentioned above, reduce the burden you placed on your victims; in other words, you must begin to make amends.

Developing Empathy

Depending on your own life experiences, you may or may not know what it feels like to be a victim. Maybe you already think about the people you've directly victimized. It is critical to your progress that you look at and understand how your illegal behavior affected them and then rippled out to affect many people. Developing empathy is a good place to start, and is incredibly important. Empathy is the ability to see things from someone else's point of view and appreciate their thoughts and feelings. Empathy is a lot more than just some clinical assessment or personal acknowledgement of another's thoughts or feelings; when you are truly empathetic, there's a kind of transference – to some extent you feel as they do.

By putting yourself in your victims' shoes, you try to imagine what your victims experienced because of your behavior. Developing empathy will allow you to actually feel someone else's fear, pain, and disappointment. You must ask yourself,

"How would I feel if I were that person?" You may feel a sense of sadness, grief, and shame as you consider the harm you've caused others; this is a healthy and natural sign that you are developing empathy for your victims. If you are struggling with the idea of empathy, think about it this way: How would you feel if someone you care about was a victim of the same crime you committed? You will come to be honestly sorry that you committed a crime (this sorrow is good – it will provide a bonus incentive to accomplish the changes you've committed to make).

The Ripple Effect

As you begin to change your lifestyle and live by positive values, you need to and must desperately want to understand and accept responsibility for the harm you have caused others by your criminal behavior. You cannot be successful otherwise. Often, the greatest harm is done to the direct victims of your crimes, but many others suffer, too, because the ripple effect from your crimes is broad and damaging. As the ripple from your crime travels outward, others besides your direct victim are affected – sometimes immediately, like your victim's family, sometimes later, like your victim's daughter who won't get to college because of lost financial support. In addition to your direct victim, your ripple effect reaches your victim's family members and friends, your family, your community, and you.

The Impact on Your Victims

It is necessary that you mentally put yourself in the position you put your victims in. Was there terror? Great pain? Do you think maybe their lives "flashed before their eyes," as the saying is? Do you suppose they thought about dying (even if they didn't) and felt sadness at missing the growing up of their children, or saying a last "I've always loved you!" to their wives? Do you suppose they thought about God and worried that they weren't ready to go? Do you suppose they developed (or would have developed, or that their family will develop) a great hate for you, a hate that will affect their lives forever, a great festering burden? And there's lots more of these sorts of questions you might think about for every victim that your ripple effect touched.

Although you cannot feel exactly as they did, you can get a sense of how you impacted their lives. If you have held resentments towards others for what they did you you, then you can begin to have an idea of the pain, fear, and damage you have done to your victims, to every victim caught in the ripple. Yes, you have to not only consider how the harm from your actions directly affected your immediate victim, but also remember that the effects of your crime have rippled out. In your review, focus on the impact you have had on each of the several groups of victims that you have harmed:

1) The impact on your victim's family.

People are connected to each other. When you hurt someone, you harm those who care about him or her, or depend on him or her. Your victim may have a spouse who will be very much hurt by any serious crime against her husband, especially one that leaves him dead or disabled physically or mentally. Children will lose opportunity when a parent's income is lost or diminished.

Parents and children suffer when family life is disrupted by your crimes.

2) The impact on your victim's extended family.

Every person is loved by a whole family tree of relatives: mothers, fathers, sisters, brothers, sons, daughters, grandparents, and so on. When someone is hurt, all these people's lives are disrupted, their emotions intensified, their duties increased, their time taken away. Family members will be obligated by family ties to provide emotional support for each other, for the victim; maybe they'll have to provide substantial financial assistance to cover family expenses, medical costs, education, who knows? They may become angry, demand justice, etc., get all roiled up inside – we all know this is not good for our health or mind. You have to think about all these people, too.

3) The impact on your family.

What a great shock of dismay, disbelief, and disappointment must visit every member of a family where a son or daughter or husband or wife has been arrested and then incarcerated for a serious crime. When it comes to family, whatever happens to one member affects the entire family, and the extended family, too. Each of them will have to adjust their lives to some extent, the closest family most of all. Every bit of the support described above for the victim's family may be required also from your family, for each other and for you. The whole family, even in distant places, may suffer from the catcalls of critics who think one bad apple means the whole family is rotten. Your situation generates strong emotions in the people who care about you. Because they suffer disruption and personal pain, they are also victims of your crime. You gave it no thought: you had no intention to harm them, but you did.

4) The impact on your community.

You belong to a number of communities, as did your victim. We're not just talking city or town here, we're talking about groups of people, all the different kinds of people that surround you and support you on the streets.

Did the victim's church hold special services? Did a public defender take your case? Did a food bank feed your family? Did the police officer processing the scene feel disgust? Did a mother turn her child away when the news covered your crime? Did some youth think that what you did must have been brave, or exciting, or at least attention-getting, and decide to emulate you? Were hospitals involved? These are just a few of the myriad ways you may have affected your communities, not to mention the possibility that many others felt terrified even though not threatened, changing their lifestyle partly or completely just to avoid meeting someone like you. All these things need to make you feel terrible, and give you the incentive you need to make the necessary amends, as much as possible.

5) The impact on you.

You probably don't consider yourself a victim of your own crime. Most people in the public won't buy into that either, and it severely limits opportunities for resuming life after release. That's one of the things that makes you a victim – your future opportunities are curtailed, reduced.

As for now, what's going on? Oh, yes; you're in prison. Your crime put you there. In at least some sense, that makes you a victim of yourself. And now, to get out, you have to do what you should have done long ago, and that is become a law-abiding person, i.e., change is needed. Granted, there are lots of inmates who really never had a chance due to childhood situations, but there are also a lot who with many or at least sufficient advantages chose to deviate. In fact, there are a bunch of inmates who had been "good" people for a long time (or seemed to be), who for some reason (anger, money, alcohol hate) succumbed to the temptation or instant non-thought opportunity to become criminal.

Your victimhood, however, is unlike the others. You'd better not feel sorry for yourself, and you certainly don't want to brag about it before the Board, but you do have to deal with yourself. A section below discusses this self-healing requirement.

Making Amends

The end of the last section said you need to deal with yourself – you will do that by dealing in some way with those you have harmed. To start with, you must be willing to start the healing process, to reach out, ask forgiveness, make restitution when possible, and promote closure. You have affected the lives of many people, and now is the time to stand up with courage and show such progress in your program of change that you prove you are becoming a decent and respectable person. The key to making amends is your willingness to act responsibly by taking full responsibility and being accountable for your actions and behavior, both then and now.

There is not a victim who does not deserve amends; there has not been any damage you've caused no deserving of restitution. At a great distance in time, and with victim's families likely not wanting anything to do with you, reaching out to make amends is difficult if not impossible, and is sometimes forbidden. Institutional regulations and some outside groups have worked out ways to permit, sometimes, a minimal at-a-distance connection between you and your victims, so you can offer sincere, sorrowful apology and seek their forgiveness. Direct contact is almost certainly out – attempts to make such contact may even result in additional charges, depending on the original crime.

To find out what you can do from where you are, you should attend and complete any available victim awareness self-help groups. You should pay careful attention in all your other self-help groups, because they probably all touch on the subject. These may reveal to you how much you can do, and how to do it. (In California, the Life Support Alliance has a class they will bring to your prison if suitable arrangements are made; it deals particularly with letters of remorse as part of its victim awareness content.) The very fact that you are attending these classes, and hopefully making some of your book study be on the subject, is a part of the amends you are making.

Any victim awareness course will likely discuss amends (apology) letters, i.e., letters of remorse. You probably shouldn't try to write one without some training, and not immediately, either; you probably can't write a good letter with or without training until you've achieved the empathy and understanding discussed previously. After you have your letter or letters, you might be able to send them in the direction of your victims by contacting the State's victims' services department; their practice is to then reach out to the victim or victim's family and see if they are willing to receive the letter. In any case, you should include the letters you write in the material you present to the Board, with an explanation of what happened to it.

There are no doubt additional ways to show remorse and make amends, but the last one discussed here is the restitution that the court ordered you to pay as part of your sentence. You should accept money from your family honestly, directly, and not indirectly. The institution will deduct some percentage of all you receive from outside, and some percentage of what you earn inside, toward your restitution. If you attempt to evade the deduction, you are not truly trying to make amends. You'll want to make sure your family is in accord with the fact that some of the money they send is never in your hands.

In a sense, you can make amends by adopting and exercising your new positive behaviors; you can continue to help make things right by not hurting others, and doing your best to be a role model for your family members and friends.

Self-Healing

Accepting responsibility and achieving a deep, remorseful appreciation for the suffering you caused does not mean that you must be in an emotional downer eternally. You may feel a sense of grief as you consider the impact of your actions; this is a healthy and natural emotion, part of gaining awareness of others' pain and grief, and the proper influence this awareness has on you. You will want to accept and work through your grief, feelings of guilt, etc., so you can move on with your life. You've recognized that your ability to make positive changes in your behavior today depends on your recognition of any past criminal behavior, and your acceptance of responsibility for it, and for its ripple of harm to many. This recognition and responsibility will allow you to understand that you are progressing along your change path. The process of healing may be slow, but you just need to remember that, in a sense, you are no longer the person who committed the crime. Of course, you can't take that literally to the Board, but you need to understand that while you're still the physical body that committed the crime, and that you will always be remorseful, you can forgive yourself and experience personal acceptance and peace.

It's time to open the door wide for genuine understanding, a healing process, and ultimately forgiveness and closure. This is proof of your willingness to grow and to acknowledge your faults, mistakes, or gross wrongs that brought harm, injury, and destruction to others without cause or justification. You are now learning about living in remorse for your victims.

CHAPTER 15

Understanding Feelings

This chapter takes a deeper look at the role your feelings play in problem behaviors. You will explore the link between thoughts, feelings, and behaviors and consider proven strategies to help you handle difficult feelings. Here, you have an opportunity to learn more about what causes you to feel a certain way and practice strategies for managing those feelings you find to be difficult. This chapter will give you an opportunity to explore how your feelings can influence your overall wellness. Consider some facts about feelings.

• Identify which of your feelings are the most challenging for you right now.

• Explore strategies for managing difficult feelings, which could include preparing for them, changing them, and/or taking action against them.

• Apply and practice these strategies you have learned to manage your difficult feelings.

Facts About Feelings

Much research has been done about why people experience certain feelings at various times and how they can adjust their feelings by changing the way they think. Feelings have a strong influence on how people behave in all types of circumstances. Some people find it difficult to recognize their feelings – and when they do, uncomfortable feelings may be difficult to accept or express. Other people may try to hide from their feelings, cover them up, or cope with them in ways that lead to life challenges.

Before you explore you own feelings and what you choose to do about them, you will want to know some general facts about the role feelings play in people's lives. Keep the following facts about feelings in mind as you start thinking about your own efforts toward wellness:

• Everyone experiences difficult feelings.

Self-talk – how people think and what they say to themselves – influences how they feel.

• Feelings influence how people behave. Feelings can come in combinations.

• People don't "make" others feel a certain way.

Difficult Feelings

Sometimes it's easy to believe you are the only one who experiences a difficult or negative feeling. Difficult feelings, such as anger, grief, and sadness, enter most people's lives at one point or another. The ups and downs of daily living present everyone with challenging experiences and exposure to contrary beliefs, which can lead to difficult feelings.

People often express difficult feelings in unhealthy ways. The way you decide to express your feelings is personal to you. While others may be able to guess how you are feeling by your appearance or from the things you say, only you know for sure what emotions you are experiencing. There is no "special" or "right" way to express difficult feelings. You do not need to mimic someone else's method of expression, nor do you need to feel like you have to share your emotions until you are ready.

Self-Talk

Your self-talk (how you think and what you say to yourself) leads to the way you feel about whatever is going on in your life. It acts like a filter between an event and how you feel about that event. This self-talk helps you interpret what's going on, based on beliefs you have established over the course of your life. It's like a little voice inside of you that is providing you with opinions and ideas. Thinking and feeling can be confusing for anyone. You and everyone else have a constant stream of "self-talk" going on in your minds all of the time.

Knowing you want to change is one thing, but how to go about it is another.

In order to change your feelings, you first have to start practicing more positive self-talk and work on some strategies that would make you feel more confident and in control. The actions you take each day are closely related to how you are feeling. Practicing positive self-talk can lead to more constructive feelings; in turn, constructive feelings – even if they are challenging to manage – are what lead to more constructive, healthy behaviors.

Change Your Self-Talk

Just because a thought comes into your head does not mean you have to keep it playing. One simple strategy you can try is stopping your thoughts. When you catch yourself thinking thoughts that cause you trouble, STOP! Don't continue following thoughts that lead you in the wrong direction. Stopping your thoughts is about turning off the fuel. This "stopping" approach will allow you to replace your old self-talk with more positive thoughts. Negative thoughts are fuel for fire. Anger, for example, is like fire. It needs new fuel to keep burning; take way the fuel and it quickly dies.

Resentful thoughts are also particularly flammable. Resentment involves blaming someone else for part of your current situation. The more you think bitter and resentful thoughts, the angrier you are likely to feel. Anxiety works in much the same way, except it is fueled by worry. If you keep fretting about unpleasant things that might happen, you are likely to feel the flame of fear in your belly.

Combinations of Feelings

You may find it quite easy to identify and label how you are feeling at a specific time. At other times, you might find it difficult or confusing to put a name to your feelings. This confusion often results when two or more emotions occur at the same time. The simultaneous feelings you experience may even seem opposed to each other. For example, you might feel sadness and anger about ending a relationship, but you might also be experiencing relief at the same time.

Everyone experiences a combination of feelings at one point or another. Often, these multiple emotions reveal themselves when people start to question what they are really feeling and how to respond. Don't let this sort of confusion bother you much – it's a good thing that you are asking questions and trying to understand. Just tolerate multiple feelings; worrying doesn't help. What you must watch for carefully, however, is that you don't let this damage your self-talk, or lead to actions you'll regret; if you allow your feelings, or any confusion about your feelings, to get in the way of making responsible decisions using your feelings as an excuse for inexcusable actions, you again create problems for you and those close to you.

Be Your Own Coach

Achieving more positive behaviors depends on choosing healthy responses to your feelings. One strategy that can help you accept, cope with, or change those emotions is being your own coach, putting YOU in control of YOU. If you blame others for your feelings, it places control in the hands of another person; you lose your ability and your responsibility to make healthy changes to how you feel. As your own coach, when there is a change you would like to make, run through it in your thoughts; consider how you can do it successfully; practice your new thoughts and behaviors mentally.

Feelings are part of being human. It is normal to experience feelings of resentment, sadness, anger, etc. With your "inner coach" in control and writing your playbook, you know in advance and have practiced what you want to do in all kinds of situations. For example, if you feel anxious in social situations, your inner coach might remind you of your self-training: "Keep good eye contact and smile. Ask about the other person – most people love to talk about themselves. Relax and get to know this person."

Mental Relaxation

The "relaxation response" is a naturally occurring altered state of consciousness that you can achieve by practicing a simple method, shown below. You might think of relaxation as doing nothing – "kicking back" – but it is also doing something – a skill. Being able to relax at various times in the day will help you manage or make changes to how you feel.

The four steps are:
1) find a quiet place; get away from as many sources of noise and distraction as possible;
2) find a comfortable position; choose one that minimizes muscle tension and that you can maintain for at least twenty minutes without moving;

3) choose something to focus your attention on; with eyes open, you could focus your gaze on a particular spot - a picture, any object, or a blank wall; with your eyes closed, you could focus on your slow and natural breathing; and
4) keep your mind clear; if thoughts, memories, or feelings drift into your awareness, just let them pass like clouds; don't hold onto them, but also don't try to keep them out. Keep bringing your attention back to your breathing or whatever you are focusing on.

During those twenty minutes, don't even think about not thinking about anything – you're not supposed to think about anything, not even about changing feelings, etc. However, afterward you'll be refreshed and your mind a little (or maybe a lot) clearer; that's the time to do your self-inspection and "coaching."

Always remember the importance of your feelings: they affect your more conscious thoughts and even your behaviors.

CHAPTER 16

Relapse Prevention

You need to know about relapse prevention for two very important reasons. First, when you go before the Board, they will want to see a relapse prevention plan; your plan must help them be confident that you won't be coming back to prison (they are a little embarrassed when they make a wrong decision). You'll need to know about relapse prevention to prepare a good plan. Second... well, you don't want to come back to prison, either. You must prepare to avoid or overcome the outside-world hazards (triggers) that lead to relapse into anger problems, drug abuse, and criminal activity. This chapter provides information to help you stay in control and avoid relapse by helping you realize when you may be slipping back into your old ways, and by helping to find better ways to respond.

Anger

It is important to have a relapse prevention plan for anger (for every problem) when you go before the Board, but you should not rely on your written plan alone. The Board will question you about your plan, and they'll ask "what if" questions. You need to read, reflect, and seek out groups or correspondence courses to help you understand and address your anger; the information below will be very helpful.

You'll need to know what are your triggers of anger. To find these, you must first identify situations that triggered your anger. Triggers are situations or conditions in your past that led to your anger, and which may do so again in the present or future.

1) To determine your triggers, it is helpful to think about your life before your anger became out of control.

2) Now, think about a situation that made you extremely angry. You may have experienced this situation many times, and you probably let your anger get out of control.

3) Looking at your life, think of five of those situations or conditions that led to you losing your ability to control your anger. These are your "triggers" – make a list of them; you'll want to include this list in your relapse prevention plan.

4) When did you decide to stop letting your anger control you? How did you do it?

5) Looking at why you took control of your anger, list five reasons why you want to stay in control.

6) What lessons from your past rehabilitative programming did you use to identify your triggers for anger?

Warning Signs of a Relapse

These common warning signs will help you identify whether a relapse is coming: Apprehension about well-being: lacking confidence in your own ability to control your anger. This can happen when you are in an aggravating situation and have difficulty in controlling yourself.

• Defensiveness: defending yourself when talking about your problems. This can happen when you don't want to accept that you are returning to your former anger.

• Crisis Building: feeling overwhelmed and unable to handle life. You may feel as if every time you deal with a life problem, two more problems appear. This might occur if your parole plans fail or are too ambitious, causing stress.

• Immobilization: feeling like you are just going through the motions of life and not really engaging with the people around you. You may feel like none of your problems can be solved, and instead spend all of your time day-dreaming.

• Plans begin to fail: no longer following through with your plans for healthy living. This can happen when you feel that your plans are too difficult.

• Irritation: feeling on the edge of your anger, being quick to lose your temper, and over-reacting to minor slights. This can happen as a result of your own frustration with yourself, or having unrealistic expectations of others.

• Depression: losing interest in things that you used to enjoy. Depression results in lethargy and a loss of daily structure. The most common symptoms of depression are irregular sleeping and eating habits.

• Loss of ability to control behavior: not attending meetings, rejecting offers of help, missing work or appointments, and/or manifesting an "I don't care" attitude. You may feel as though being ineffective in your ability to remain in control of your anger means you are an ineffective person.

• Conscious lying: finding yourself explaining away the truth of your situation and instead believing lies about yourself.

Now that you can identify warning signs, you need a plan for dealing with them. Here are some examples of possible elements of your plan:
• Attend a meeting
• Talk with your sponsor
• Think of your daily inventory. What are your priorities? Why are you committed to your changes?
• Take ten seconds to breathe and reassess the situation.

- Call a supportive friend.
- Relax. Engage in a relaxing activity that you enjoy.
- If you are a person of faith, pray; invite like-minded friends to pray with you or for you.

Substance Abuse, AA/NA (12 Steps)

This information defines substance addiction and provides a better understanding of the effect that alcohol and other drugs have on your body, your mind, and your life. There are official definitions for alcoholism and drug addiction, but the easiest way of describing a substance-related disorder may be by thinking of riding a roller coaster. The ride occurs when you experience problems from the use of mood-altering chemicals, but fail to change your using behavior.

You may not connect your use of alcohol or drugs with the problems that result from their use. You may deny that your financial, family, health, or legal problems are consequences of drinking or using drugs. As time goes on, you become more focused on getting high and recovering from the substance as your roller coaster gets more out of control. You ride up on a chemical high and come crashing down with physical, emotional, and social consequences of your use.

Now is a good time to get off that roller coaster and work toward a more responsible way of life. The information here will help you. You will want to address your substance abuse behaviors as a priority. Although you may face other challenges at times, it is in your best interest to put your substance abuse problems as your top priority, because substance addiction can lead to:

1) Chronic disease: a chronic disease progresses slowly, is constant, and lasts for a long period of time. Chronic diseases include diabetes, heart disease, emphysema, and arthritis.

2) The disease progressing: diseases are seductive and persistent. If the substance abuse goes unchecked, the

substance-addicted person moves from an early stage where the substance appears helpful to an uncontrollable craving to the later stages of the disease, when the addicted person's body starts to give up.

Many physical problems arise. The substance-addicted person's mental, emotional, and spiritual strength is sapped. Because the disease is progressive, the condition becomes more severe over time.

3) Death: if a person continues to abuse his or her substance, the addiction can lead to early death as a result of

• Liver, heart, kidney, pancreas, or lung failure;
• Overdose;
• Suicide; or
• Auto, water, fire, or other type of accident.

Recovery and change is possible for anyone who takes their recovery and change seriously. Through the support of groups, correspondence courses, and the helpful guidance of a sponsor, you can begin to change your attitude.

Choices, and decisions. Recovery is a process requiring patience, commitment, and practical application of the 12 Steps as taught by AA and NA.

Illegal Activity and Gang Involvement

Illegal activity and gang involvement are also addictive behaviors that you may have developed. These destructive addictions have to be addressed and dealt with just as any other addiction would be. The odds of success have long been – against anyone involved with illegal activity or gangs. If you're in prison, it's most likely behind one or both of these issues. But you can change and use your past as a stepping stone to success.

Illegal activity and gang involvement can be better known as "lifestyle addictions." These addictions are usually rooted in a negative way of thinking and living. You became involved with illegal activity and gangs because your beliefs and pride were fueled by traditions.

When entering a recovery process, it's important to admit there is a problem. Your past is full of facts you cannot deny. If you've been involved with illegal activity and gangs throughout your life, you're most likely addicted to that way of life. Addiction is not simply a habit, though addicts tend to think of their repeated behaviors as "only a habit," a self-lie, implying a belief it can be easily set aside. A habit is something you repeat over and over that has become automatic, perhaps even unconscious. Addiction goes beyond that: addiction has no conscience, nor compassion; addiction is lethal, self-serving, and always craves something.

The addiction – no matter to what choice of illegal activity, whether theft, drug dealing, violence, gang involvement, substance abuse, etc. – starts in your mind with what is called an obsession. This obsession should not be mistaken for a normal thought. It is human nature to think, and thoughts come and go moment by moment. An obsession greatly differs because it is a persistent, nagging idea, desire, or emotional rush that you can't seem to get rid of and within this obsession, you become isolated in one or more of these components of the obsession:

1) A persistent IDEA that you want or need something, and you convince yourself that you deserve it, that you are too smart to get caught, and that it is only this one time, that it is not a habit.

2) A persistent DESIRE that you want or need something, and you convince yourself that you deserve it, that you that you are too smart to get caught, and that you only want it once, that it is not a habit.

3) A persistent EMOTIONAL RUSH that you want or need to do something, and you convince yourself that you deserve

it, that you are too smart to get caught, and that you only want it once, that it is not a habit.

Lifestyle problems are driven by the power of addiction; you've come to understand the cycle of addition, and you've come to realize there is a need to change. You know change is possible, and you believe that being responsible for yourself will make change happen. You look back on your past to identify your pattern of behavior (a regular way of acting or doing something) that was illegal. You gave yourself permission to commit a crime by convincing yourself you needed something, you deserved it, and you could get away with it.

The addiction is the reason you commit a crime repeatedly, and the crime itself is some illegal act that you enjoy for self-gratification. The cycle of addiction is powerful because it has three components (parts) that work together:

1) OBSESSION: This is a persistent idea, desire, or emotion that cannot be got rid of by normal reasoning.

2) COMPULSION: This is an irresistible driving force to perform some illegal act, and once the irrational impulse has started, it repeats over and over.

3) PROGRESSION: This is the fact that your criminal behavior moves forward, continuing by successive steps, getting worse and out of control.

The addiction proves its strength and control over you in three main ways:

1) You damage or destroy almost all relationships with family, friends, co-workers, and those in the public.

2) You become an extremely irresponsible person, blaming others, and making excuses to avoid getting help for your problems.

3) Any spiritual, moral, or ethical beliefs or practices are blocked and disregarded altogether during the time frame

when addiction is active; you are locked in a tunnel view of committing a crime and gaining satisfaction.

It is always one or more of the components of obsession (idea, desire, or emotional rush) that pushes you to give yourself permission to move directly into the compulsion stage of the addiction cycle; compulsion immediately and inevitably follows the obsession, and soon gives over to irresistible action.

Once you act, you are sure to repeat doing whatever crime you committed. Sometimes you will repeat within days or weeks, but for sure you will repeat, because the obsession will return to your mind again, strong and powerful.

Each time you act out illegally, you lack the ability to control your behavior rationally. Once you commit the crime and justify repeating it, you will begin to do the crime over and over more frequently. This is what you find as the third stage of the addiction cycle, known as progression.

You will persistently repeat a crime, or a series of crimes, so often that you are out of control and your problem with illegal activity has progressively gotten worse. It is the vicious cycle you cannot take for granted as you journey through the change process.

Obsession, Compulsion, Progression and Relapse Prevention

The description of addiction makes the situation look ugly, like you can't escape. It's tough, true enough, but remember that it's the addiction cycle that is ugly, not you as a human. You will learn to separate the two – addiction and yourself – as you go through the recovery process. So, what can you do to incorporate the cycle of addiction to criminal activity into your relapse prevention plan? The answer must come in two parts.

In prison, are you caught up already in a cycle like this? Have you convinced yourself, for example, that you deserve that pruno, so just this once, you'll make some, you won't get caught, and maybe you'll get a little money on the side? You now can recognize instantly what's going on. What else might qualify? Do you have to be first in the shower, reserve a table, stand grand? More of the same. You've already relapsed. How do you break the cycle? You hang around with different people, you honor your commitments to AA, NA, and other self-help programs. It's a matter of self-discipline, and given the nature of addiction, it will be tough. You will need help; seek it and use it – the prison's main job is to get you past these addictions. Many are stupid and want to be just the same when they go as when they came; don't be one of them.

As to what will happen when you leave prison, the Board will be extremely interested in what led to your particular crime, and what you understand about it. Your understanding is part of what they call "insight", and if you can't convince them you've gained insight, they'll be more than happy to give you a few (maybe many) more years to figure things out. They will have identified for themselves already some of what they think got you involved in crime. It's best if you've spotted these things for yourself before they ask you. Did you hang around with people who were already criminals? Did you get hooked on drugs and need lots of money? Did you take advantage of weak people? Did you think some people wouldn't miss a little bit, or mind that you took advantage of a weakness, maybe thought they actually enjoyed being victimized? You need to admit any of this to the Board, and in your relapse prevention plan talk about how you'll recognize any urges, maintain the absence of addiction (since you'll be claiming you got rid of it in prison), and what steps you'll be taking to avoid getting caught up again in a criminal lifestyle.

CHAPTER 17

Self-Help in Prison

You should understand by now how important it is to get involved with self-help. Self-help comes in many different forms, such as groups, correspondence courses, and books. Not only will these studies help you GET OUT, they will help you STAY OUT ... that's a win-win! They help you prepare for the Parole Board and help you better yourself as a person; both are very important. Using the information and resources listed here can help you to be productive and effective in your personal self-help programming.

Self-Help Groups

The self-help groups you attend in prison promote positive life change. So, if you haven't started yet, it's about time to begin the process of self-change. Changing behavior is not easy; your success depends upon your motivation and effort. This process will serve you best when you're honest with yourself. Groups help enable this honesty. By applying the valuable information you will be learning from attending groups to your own situation, you will begin to develop your personal roadmap to success.

The groups you'll attend are programs that offer you the opportunity to learn the skills necessary to live a life free of violence and abuse of any kind.

Most people are not excited about attending groups; you may feel angry or embarrassed. You may feel like you don't belong in the group at all. Those are normal feelings.

You will benefit most from the group experience if you are willing to explore the choices that led you to prison and honestly express your thoughts and feelings about your current situation. Being part of a group may be new to you, but it's important to understand that others in the group share some of the same challenges as you. Of course, it may be difficult to take responsibility for the choices you've made and the harm you've caused others, but in order to promote positive life change, these are the things you'll have to do.

To make the most of group experiences, you are encouraged to give input along the way. Feel free to share your ideas and your feedback. If you want to make positive changes in your life, it's up to you to participate, do the work, apply the skills you learn, and give support to others who want to change. Sharing your experiences with others is a big part of being in a group. When everyone is willing to listen and share, everybody in the group benefits. You should always respect the confidentiality of your group members. What is shared within the group, stays in group.

Regardless of what groups your prison offers, it's important to get involved with all the groups that are offered to you. In some prisons, you might expect to actually be assigned to a group-like class or series of meetings, like Transitions, or Drug Awareness Programming, etc. Often, membership in a group is by assignment even if you are volunteering; for example, AA and NA often are full; you'll need to get on a waiting list by talking to the group's sponsor or to your counselor.

The Five Steps of Change

While in prison, you will learn and practice skills to help you successfully change away from your past behavior. Learning about the five steps of change will help you understand why some people successfully make changes the first time, while others eventually return to their unhealthy ways. To improve your chances of success in changing your harmful behaviors, take time to learn the five steps of change, given below.

Change doesn't happen overnight. So when you find yourself taking positive steps forward, you might find yourself going back a step. Even though this can be frustrating, you can learn from the experience. Each time you go back a step, get back on track. This is all part of the change process, and how real change takes place.

STEP 1: NOT INTERESTED
In this step, you don't feel the need to change. You don't feel that your attitudes and behaviors create problems. You can't be motivated to change harmful attitudes and behaviors if you don't know you have them.

STEP 2: INTERESTED IN CHANGE
You may be unsure about where you need to change. You may like your life as it is, yet know it could be better if you made some changes. If you are struggling with what to do, that's okay; consider it a good sign. This is natural when you are thinking about change.

STEP 3: PREPARING FOR CHANGE
This step gets you ready to make a change in your behavior. You start to focus on how you can make changes. You look into your options, make some hard decisions, and commit to changing.

139

STEP 4: TAKING ACTION

You start changing the way you think, the things you say, and the way you conduct yourself. You may feel uncomfortable while changing old habits, but as you practice your new habits, you will gradually feel more comfortable. Focus on taking action today.

STEP 5: STICKING WITH IT

By the time you've reached this step, you have come a long way in your journey. You've made positive changes to your behavior and are focused on not slipping back into your old ways.

Now that you know the steps, take some time and determine where you are today. Then work towards taking more steps forward. Your behavior sets an example for others; so, do you want to be a negative influence, or would you rather have a positive impact on the people around you.

Changing your behavior for the better can improve the way you feel about yourself and the life you live. For people in prison, there are many self-help groups, correspondence courses, books, and other resources available for those who want to change. Should you happen to be housed where the programs are not available, or you prefer to seek outside assistance, it is available, as well.

Options for Correspondence Courses and Books

Listed below are correspondence courses and books that you may find helpful in your program of change, whether or not you participate in groups. Inclusion in the lists does not represent any endorsement of the programs and books, but they are general suggestions. It is a place you can start – especially if there are no prison groups available to you - but please do not limit yourself to this list. Some of the courses and books might work for you, others might not. It's up to you to find what works for your journey.

Correspondence Courses:

• 12-STEP PROGRAMS: Alcoholics Anonymous (AA) is often offered at prisons. If it's not available at your prison, it's possible to start (or continue) the program via mail. You can write to General Service Office, P.O. Box 459, Grand Central Station, New York, NY 10163.
• CREATIVE OPTIONS: This is a correspondence course that offers lessons on Parenting, 12-Step Programming, Anger Management, Adult Children of Alcoholics, and Journals for Healing. Write to Creative Options, P.O. Box 808, Lyons, OR 97358. BEHIND THE WALLS: This is a sponsorship program that will assist you in working the 12 steps of Narcotics Anonymous by assigning you a recovering addict to be your sponsor through correspondence. Write to Central California Region BTWS, P.O. Box 1206, Ventura, CA 93002-1206.
• LOVE LIFTED ME RECOVERY: Request their 12-step recovery correspondence courses. Write to Love Lifted Me Recovery, Tom and Dottie Hooper, P.O. Box 10966, Marina Del Ray, CA 90295.
• GETTING OUT BY GOING IN (GOGI): A positive prison culture created by prisoners for prisoners. Some prisons have in-person groups, and there are also correspondence courses in Anger Management, Insight Development, and others.
Write to Getting Out By Going In (GOGI), P.O. Box 88969, Los Angeles, CA 90009.
• HOUSES OF HEALING: A program for emotional literacy that offers guidance in understanding causative factors, taking responsibility, and changing patterns of violence and addiction. Some prisons have in-person groups,

and correspondence options might be available. Write to The Lionheart Foundation, P.O. Box 170115, Boston, MA 02117

• PARTNERSHIP FOR REENTRY PROGRAM (PREP): This is a program run for inmates in California by Sister Mary Sean Hodges. Many of the volunteers who help run the program are ex-Lifers. The program includes correspondence courses on many different topics. You can also take a special module on "insight" that includes mock parole hearings. Write to PREP/TURNING POINT, P.O. Box 77850, Los Angeles, CA 90007.

• CRIMINON WEST US: Greg Capazorio, the president of this organization, has worked with staff from prisons all over the world. If you want or need material for self-help, they offer multiple courses. Criminon pays for everything (books, worksheets, correspondence, postage to mail the material, etc.). They take time, but are good courses. Write to Criminon West US, P.O. Box 9091, Glendale, CA 91226.

• PRISON LETTERS 4 OUR STRUGGLING YOUTH: Request to join their letter-writing campaign to help detour our struggling youth from a life of crime, drugs, and gangs. Ask for the "Binding Agreement" to get started. They will fax letters to the Board for each letter you write, and will send you a copy for your file. Write to B.A.B.Y. Prison Letter, 5742 Crenshaw Blvd. Suite 562, Los Angeles, CA 90043.

• BEHAVIORAL SYSTEMS: Request a list of the correspondence courses. Write to Behavioral Systems Southwest, Inc., Hollywood Reentry, 1831 N. Vine St., Hollywood, CA 90028

• CROSSROADS: This organization offers a Bible study correspondence course that connects people in prison with volunteer mentors in Christ-centered relationships that transform lives and prisons. Write to Crossroads Prison Ministries, P.O. Box 900, Grand Rapids, MI 49509-0900.

• AMAZING GRACE: This is an eight-lesson home Bible study course that will survey some of the most important

aspects of Bible teaching. Write to Amazing Grace International, P.O. Box 8453, Falls Church, VA 22041.
• WELS: This is a Bible study course that has 22 Bible-study booklets. After they receive each "final test", they will send you another booklet. Write to WELS Special Ministries, P.O. Box 452, New Ulm, MN 56073.

BOOKS BY TOPIC:

ANGER -
• *Beyond Anger* by Thomas Harbin
• *Letting Go of Anger* by Ronald Potter-Efron
• *Rage: Step By Step to Overcoming Explosive Anger* by Ronald Potter-Efron
• *Anger Among Angels* by William DeFoore
• *The Anger Trap* by Dr. Les Carter
• *Cage Your Rage: An Inmate's Guide to Anger Control* by Murray Cullen

SUBSTANCE ABUSE -
• *Understanding the 12 Steps* by Terence Gorski
• *Staying Sober* by Terence Gorski
• *Selfish Brain: Learning From Addiction* by Robert L. DuPont
• *Passages Through Recovery* by Terence Gorski
• *Enough Already: A Guide to Recovery From Alcohol and Drug Addiction* by Bob Tyler'
• *AA: The Big Book*
• *NA: It Works How and Why*

MISCELLANEOUS -
• *Change Your Questions, Change Your Life* by Marilee Adams
• *Writing My Wrongs* by Shaka Senghor

143

- *Little Book of Restorative Justice For People In Prison* by Barb Toews
- *How to Break your Addiction to a Person* by Howard M. Haip-em, Ph.D.
- *The Power of Intention* by Wayne Dyer
- *Man's Search for Meaning* by Viktor Franki
- *Path to Peace* by Shi Wuling
- *The Secret* by Rhoda Bryne
- *For One More Day* by Mitch Alborn
- *Think and Grow Rich* by Napoleon Hill
- *Unlimited Power* by Anthony Robbins

FREE BOOKS -

- HUMAN KINDNESS FOUNDATION: For free books and newsletters, write to Human Kindness Foundation, P.O. Box 60619, Durham, NC 27715.
- PRISONERS' LITERATURE PROJECT: They have been sending free books to prisoners for over 30 years. Write to Prisoners' Literature Project c/o Bound Together Bookstore, 1369 Haight Street, San Francisco, CA 94117.
- THE PRISON LIBRARY PROJECT: They provide books to prisoners. Request topics. Write to The Prison Library Project, 915-CW, Foothill Blvd., PMB 128, Claremont, CA 91711-3356.

PART FOUR:

STAY OUT! PREPARING FOR RELEASE

If you are like most convicts, you've spent many years in prison thinking about what freedom will be like when you get out. Unfortunately, without preparing for life outside of prison, even the most optimistic can stumble and end up back in prison. So Part Four is all about helping you STAY OUT!

The purpose of Part Four is to help the people who need it the most: you who are about to be released from prison. The goal is to give hands-on advice that will provide you with the information and tools that can help you STAY OUT!

CHAPTER 18

Stay Out

In previous parts of this book, one fact has been clear – to get out of prison, you need to change yourself from enslavement to criminality to a sufficiently rehabilitated self that the Board would provide a date and you would get out.

All that advice and information was extremely important to you, a Lifer.

Here, we've reached the next step. This chapter reaffirms the need for change, as being critical for you to stay out. You don't want to join the Board in embarrassment that you've returned to prison – and you probably will, if your preparation doesn't include true change. Also, as you'll see, you'll want to continue your self-improvement after you get out.

Note that this chapter (in fact, every chapter from here on) applies to every prisoner being released – not just those that had to prove to the Board that they were ready. You can spread the word: those with fixed dates need to do all the same preparation, including that outlined in previous chapters, if they want to stay out.

How To Stay Out?

An important statistic to remember is that ex-cons who remain arrest-free for five years have a 97% chance of staying out forever!

Consider this: In order to build a life when you get out, you have to actually stay out! To achieve this, you must make the right choices at the right times and avoid a long list of possible situations such as picking up new charges, getting into domestic strife, or violating some condition of parole.

So, to help you achieve staying out, you should set yourself a goal of staying arrest-free for five years. But why five years? That's a long time! It's because when a person stays out of trouble that long, there is a great chance he or she will stay out forever. To do this, you have to learn to live by values that society will accept. This means making a commitment to positive, constructive conduct. You must live in a way that gives you the best odds of remaining arrest-free.

If you are resourceful, creative, and determined, you can interact with many wonderful people, places, and things. The good news is that the rewards for a positive, constructive way of life are great and deeply fulfilling. There's no glory in being a gangster for ten minutes, then ending up paying for it with the next ten years of your life. Or worse! So, once you're back in the world, watch yourself very, very closely. Monitor every thought, feeling, action, and decision in order to protect your freedom and improve your life. Make up your mind to be the master of your own destiny.

In prison, you have very few choices; every day is the same old routine. But in the free world, just the opposite is true. Instead of having too few things to do, you have too many... and they often compete with each other.

So you have to make constant adjustments and decisions about how to apply your time and energy.

Prepare For The Streets

The question is: How will you be one of those who get out and stay out? How are you going to increase your odds of never coming back? Your first couple of years out will be a long, hard, complicated journey, testing your endurance, determination, and ability to adapt to new situations. So your best bet is to use your last year down to prepare for your first year of freedom. I'm not talking about just the obvious survival issues, like money, employment, housing, and transportation. Don't be misled – all this matters; but true success depends even more on how you deal with the mental, emotional, and social changes that will confront you.

A word of caution: Too often, prisoners and their loved ones believe that the only problem standing between them and happiness is attaining release. But this isn't true: Release is only the midpoint of a much larger experience. Every moment of captivity must be used to prepare, so that personal fulfillment will be the final outcome.

Clearly, getting out of prison doesn't guarantee you'll stay out. However, getting out does give you the chance to actively pursue a rich and rewarding future. Getting out would be a wonderful change from your current situation. Getting out gives you the opportunity to succeed, but the burden of staying out is on you.

As you get close to getting out, identify the invisible chains that bind you and begin to break loose in a slow and orderly manner. To best prepare for the streets, you must examine your values and feelings - those that led up to your arrest as well as those you've developed while doing your time. Figure out which of them are negative and destructive, and replace them with positives. You will also realize that you have gained useful insights from the adversity you've faced; examine those also, and apply this hard-earned knowledge in constructive ways. Get one thing straight: "preparation" is far more than trying to figure out where to live, how to get a job, and what to look for in a used car. It's about deciding how you are going to deal with people and what values you are going to live by.

Better Yourself

It is time to start thinking about who you're going to be once you hit those bricks, how you intend to carry yourself and deal with those around you. Harsh as it may have been, your imprisonment is a "learning experience." You can use the power and insight gained as fuel for your progress and growth. The sooner you consciously apply that power and insight to progress and grow, the smoother your reentry to the outside world will be. Before you get out, it is important to repair and improve the ways you think and how you react to yourself and the things that go down around you. This means looking deep inside yourself, taking an honest inventory, and making every effort to fix whatever doesn't work. No one else can, will, or should do this for you; it is your right and your responsibility. In fact, it is the key to true freedom.

As you examine and redefine the things that matter to you and the person you want to become, be sure to include an honest look at the goals and ambitions you will take with you out of prison. Your success in the free world depends to a large extent on making the right choices. To do so, you need good information – true facts, not wishful thinking. Above all, you must be honest and real with yourself.

So take time to examine your expectations of the future. What is your mental picture of the first few months after your release? How do you expect other people to react to you? How do you expect to react yourself? How hard will it be to get back on your feet – to get a job, housing, transportation? How long will it take? What could go wrong?

To develop realistic plans for the future, you need a clear mind and the courage to face reality. You must work constantly to overcome false expectations and distorted thinking. By doing all you can now to bring your thoughts into line with what is real and true, you will significantly improve your chances of survival and success when you get out.

True Freedom

Remember that your goal is to be positive and constructive, not negative and disruptive. By controlling your actions you can better control your future. Your goal is to discover a path leading to maximum freedom and success, thus freeing yourself from the multitude of forces which enslave you. So take a truthful look at the thoughts and feelings that drive you.

Through this inventory process, you sort out the useful from the trash, the real from the fake. As you go along, take special note of the thoughts, feelings, and actions that consistently result in pain, shame, dishonor, anxiety, guilt, and isolation (or that did so in your past), then consider their direct opposites, such as comfort, pride, harmony, forgiveness, peace, and belonging. Study each of these positive elements very closely until you see that you do have a choice in most cases.

Practice turning the negatives around a little bit each day, both in your awareness and by actually performing small acts of "positive reversal." Try something new. Where you find fear, practice forgiveness, not to do favors for anybody else, but to move beyond the darkness of the past into the light of a positive future. Such efforts may seem too simple to do much good, but if practiced with a deliberate intent to break free from negative habits, they will improve your chances of success by a thousand percent!

Look within yourself for answers to questions such as:

150

1) How am I going to live in the future in a way that is an improvement over my past life, the things that resulted in my getting locked up?

2) How can I best take control of my fate so that I am truly in charge of my life?

3) What must I do to make amends to myself and others, for the grief and discomfort my actions have caused?

4) What is really worth living for... and what am I willing to do to achieve it? What sacrifices am I willing to make?

Your answers hold the key to true freedom: freedom from past influences and events; freedom from the chains of fear, rage, longing, and isolation; freedom from forces outside yourself that seem to control your mind and spirit.

Exploring your inner self is hard work, but well worth the effort. Your purpose is to connect with yourself, with who you are and wish to become. Through this process, you gain a growing sense of your center, your real identity as a person of worth. Only from that level of deep awareness can you really connect with the people you love and value and, ultimately, with anyone you meet in the free world.

Personal Responsibility

There is one essential reality you must grasp when preparing for the free world: You are responsible for your own life – past and present, good and bad. Once you accept that you are in fact the captain of your own ship, you realize that you have the ability to guide and improve your future by changing the ways you think and act. But it's up to you to take "ownership" of your own life and future, and the price of ownership is that you accept responsibility for who you are, what you do, and the results of your actions. Until you do this, your life doesn't truly belong to you.

This whole concept of self-responsibility, which many of us have always considered a negative burden, is in fact our greatest treasure. Rather than being a chain which binds us with guilt, shame, and punishment, it is actually the source of our freedom. It gives us the power to choose and the opportunity to reap the rewards of positive actions. You always have the ability to choose how you will handle what life throws your way.

The longer you've been locked up, the greater the rush of getting out. You will face a lot of confusion and conflicting emotions, but with time you will sort things out. Give yourself the time you need to adjust. So, as you prepare to expand control of your life, you ought to commit to three basic elements of self-control. First, realize that you are responsible for your choices and actions – not just sometimes, but always. Second, strive to base everything you think, feel, and do only that which is true, real, and fair. Third, stop and think. Refuse to be controlled by raw emotion; analyze the best way to handle the next step in any given situation.

As you focus on and practice these three things, you will gain greater power and control over your decisions and actions. And this will make your plans for the future far more real and achievable.

CHAPTER 19

Survival Plan

This chapter focuses your attention on your survival plan, outlining the information you would put into an institutional parole or release plan, if you are required to have one. If it turns out your Board doesn't need one, or the system will just release you on a date certain, remember that your life needs a survival plan. You definitely should not step foot out of prison without knowing what's likely to happen, what you plan to do if everything goes right, and what you're going to do if anything goes wrong. Remember that a useful survival plan must, above all, be practical and achievable.

Build Your Plan

A survival plan covers some basic needs: 1) a survival budget and source of essential funds; 2) employment; 3) family and personal support; 4) housing; 5) transportation; 6) legal concerns and supervision; and 8) personal development.

Each of these basic needs and the required planning is detailed in the paragraphs that follow here.

Survival

Budget and Funds

Start by developing a budget – a list of what you will need money for, how much you expect to need for each category, and when you will need it. Budgeting is a valuable skill, not just for survival, but to help you achieve your goals throughout life. So, make it a habit to update your budget regularly, both before and after you leave prison, and keep track of how you spend your money. After basic survival needs like food are met, the next major concern is start-up costs like deposits (apartment, utilities, telephone, etc.), work clothes and tools, and basic transportation. Try to postpone as many of these costs as you can for the first 90 days, until you get come cash flow going. This might include planning to stay with family or in a halfway house until you get on your feet. Use three months as a reasonable goal to be able to go out on your own.

The ideal situation is to have a nest egg that covers you for up to the first three months after release. Although very few can do this, be thinking of any legal and ethical way to have something waiting for you, no matter how little it may be. Even if it's not much, something is always better than nothing.

Employment

The best thing you could do is to take the first job you can find, even if it's not ideal, and be steadily looking for something better (do remember, though, that if you change jobs too often, it gets harder to find a new one). Of all your needs fresh out of prison, finding a job is at the top of the list. You may even need to work as temporary labor for a while to get survival funds until you find a permanent job and get a cash flow started. But don't get discouraged. Set your mind on getting a job and don't give up. The longer you keep trying, the more the odds will turn in your favor. There's more on this subject in Chapter 20.

Family and Personal Support

Your family, loved ones, friends, and associates will become your "support system." As you know, these people are your main link to the world, both in and out of prison, and the source of comfort, encouragement, and help when needed. In return for their help, you owe them your honesty, appreciation, and respect.

Nothing is more critical to your fate than the quality of your relationships, so think about who you will (and who you will not) relate to in the streets and the best ways to do it. It's better to have only a few friends on the street than to be locked up with a bunch of home boys.

Housing

Finding a place to live should always be a major part of a prisoner's release plan. People often intend to return to family, but if that option is not available, you must make other plans. One alternative - in some cases a requirement – is a halfway house. Although this may not seem like an appealing option, it does provide two of life's essentials, food and shelter. So, don't reject it right Out of the gate.

Although halfway houses and shelters are not the ideal living situation, they sure beat a prison cell or sleeping under a bridge. Many have excellent reputations and track records. They may also help with other needs such as finding a job, so appreciate them and use them for what they offer. While staying there, you can sometimes save until you have enough money for apartment rent, utilities, and deposits. You'll want to put away enough savings to cover an extra two to three month's living expenses before you make the move. There's more on this in Chapter 22.

Transportation

Unless you plan to stay in the community where you are released, transportation will probably be your first need after release. If you don't have a family member or friend to meet you, you will be using public transportation, most likely a bus. Try to find out the fare and schedule for where you need to go. The schedule is important to make sure you don't get stranded at a bus station or street corner in the middle of the night.

Until you can save enough money for a used car, you will need to use public transportation. It's possible you'll choose to not get a car, because today, most major urban areas have buses and other forms of mass transit. Get a free schedule of the routes so you can plan ahead to get where you need to be.

Healthcare

Good health is important. It affects everything you do, including your ability to prosper and enjoy your freedom. So, learn how to protect and improve your health. Good nutrition, exercise, and rest are important elements. They will also keep you mentally clear and physically fit to deal with problems and overcome the stress that accompanies release.

If you have a health problem (physical or mental) that will need attention when you return to the community, now is the time to research available help and forms of financial support. If you need regular medication, such as for diabetes, TB, hepatitis C, or an emotional illness, try to get a supply of your medication to take out with you that will last until you can make arrangements to get a prescription filled after release. If you can't get an appointment with a free-world doctor right away, look for a public health clinic or hospital that may offer the help you need.

Legal Concerns and Parole

Most people get out of prison on some kind of supervision, be it parole, federal probation, electronic monitoring, etc. Some may be required to stay in a halfway house or participate in activities such as counseling. Many also owe restitution or fines, or have to pay supervision fees or back child support. And if you have a drug history, expect to be drug tested often, and always when you least expect it. You must learn in advance the rules you will have to follow. Too many find out that messing up while under supervision can be another fast track back to prison. So stay on your toes!

You will be required to report to your parole officer very soon after release. Be sure you know when and where, and make plans for how you will get there on time. There's no point in being labeled an absconder just because you got lost or didn't have the bus fare.

Personal Development

The only way to beat the system is to outgrow it! And the best way to make life meaningful is to be in a constant state of positive change. One of the great things about getting out is that there are many more ways than in prison to make your life richer and fuller.

Many kinds of education and training opportunities are available in most areas. For those who get tired of flipping burgers, nothing is better than taking some vocational training to expand their skills and income. Some prisons also offer vocational training that you may be able to take advantage of. But learning brings fresh energy and greater self-respect.

So check out what is available in the area where you plan to be released.

Costs are often far less than you might expect. You may not be able to get involved in this type of self-advancement right after you get out; it is something to look at as a more long-term goal. But knowing the possibility is there will give you something to look forward to and remind you of the positive rewards for your hard work.

Your Action Plan

Survival plans are most useful when combined with an action plan that includes dates, times, and tasks – what you intend to do to achieve your immediate goals. It sounds simple enough to go home, relax, see your family and friends, then find a job. But in all the rush of activity and emotion, you may find your plans getting lost or confused. If you have an action plan, especially for the first few weeks of freedom, it will help you focus on what you need to do next.

Keep it simple; don't overload yourself in the first few days of freedom. Take care of essentials and leave some time to spend just getting used to things and savoring your freedom.

After You Get Out

It might take a mountain of motivation and courage, but you can make the changes needed to build a rewarding future. Above all, have faith in yourself – your efforts will pay off. Don't look at change as a threat. We often fear it because it brings uncertainty and stress, but that doesn't mean it's bad. Just the opposite: It's the promise of change that gives us hope for a better future. So set aside any fears you may have and welcome it!

Once you get out, don't seclude yourself, hiding because of shame, fear, or embarrassment, or because you don't know what to tell people about your past. Having been in prison is just an experience, one of the many experiences people go through in life. It's who you are today – as your values and actions reflect - that matters, not where you've been. After you're out for a few years, you will see that your past is no longer an issue, as it was right after you got out.

Reconnecting With Your Loved Ones

Your loved ones will be wondering who you will truly be when you get out. This cannot be answered in mere words, only through actions over time. Strive to be honest, sincere, gentle, and dependable. That's what they will value above all else.

Only time and consistent effort can reduce the discomfort that naturally comes when people come together after a long time apart. In one sense, you may feel unusually close to your loved ones due to the intensity of emotions, but in other ways you may feel like a total stranger. Now that you are finally together again, you realize that neither of you is the same as you once were or as you remember each other to be. You must allow time to get to know each other all over again.

`As you work to rebuild your relationship, it is important to realize that love is a very special relationship built on honesty, respect, shared goals, and consistency. One essential ingredient is communication; you must be honest and open when you express how you feel and be willing to listen when others share their feelings with you.

Your loved ones need to be able to trust, respect, and believe in you. Don't get upset if people express doubts about you, directly or indirectly. Remember why they have these concerns and work even harder to prove that you are on the right path. Also remember that you will have specifically asked some of your loved ones to watch out for signs of recidivism or other difficulty, and to be frank with you; take them seriously. It will take time and steady positive action to rebuild people's trust in you.

CHAPTER 20

Be Patient and Build a Foundation

People get out of prison desperate for many things, and desperate people have no patience. Fresh out, you have to start at the bottom and build a life from scratch; that means starting with a foundation – without it your future won't have anything stable to stand on. Have faith and know that if you invest enough time and effort, you will ultimately achieve the rewards you hunger for.

Build Your Foundation

A big part of coping with life after prison is coming to terms with time.

In prison, all you wanted was for your time to be over with. Now that you're out, you're anxious and impatient because time still won't let you have everything you want instantly. This desire for instant gratification comes from desperation and the illusion that you can catch up on all you've lost while doing your time. But time does not answer to anyone; you can either fight it or flow with it... one or the other!

You can save yourself a lot of grief by accepting reality: the first couple of years after you get out will be consumed by the effort of rebuilding your life. During most of this period, your main priority will be daily survival. You have to build a strong foundation on which your future will stand, solid and secure. Start with a reasonable plan and build from there, one small step at a time.

Above all, be ready to let your common sense guide you, not your emotions and wishful thinking. Celebrate even the smallest victory and give yourself time to achieve major progress. After you have your survival needs under control and your personal business in order, THEN you can make major life decisions, like opening a business, buying a house, getting married, or having a baby.

Some big dreams, like owning your own business, may be possible, but they will take even longer, and you will have to pay major dues to make them happen. Expecting to make your dreams come true in the first few months or years after prison often leads to failure and despair. Instead, use your energy to build the skills, resources, and support you need to turn your ambitions into reality.

Be Patient

As we've discussed, your first year back on the streets is an extremely critical period. The best advice on how to handle this time is to stay focused on the things you need to do to survive. To keep you on track, stick to your survival plan. It will give you a useful sense of direction during this confusing time.

First, review your short-range plans. These are your immediate goals, the practical things that will begin your journey. Be careful - don't let your list overcome you! Remember that building the foundation for your future is a slow process, so avoid taking on or expecting too much too soon. Work on a few of your most essential needs each day. Your plan will help you set priorities and decide how to apply your limited time and resources.

At the end of each day, spend thirty minutes evaluating your progress and making a schedule for your next day. When something is harder than you expected or doesn't work out as you hoped, adapt by revising your plan and readjusting your mind, energy, and resources. The keys to your success are organization, resistance, and patience. Your progress will come in small steps, each one building on the one before. You will find that even a little progress provides a feeling of growing pride and confidence.

The Five Basic Areas of Your Foundation

Before you can move forward to your long-range life plans, a variety of issues must be addressed. These fall into five basic areas of your foundation: 1) be patient; 2) surviving parole; 3) money management; 4) finding a job; and 5) staying out.

Be Patient

Time and patience will help you accept that you really are out and a part of the free world. Building a quality of life after prison demands strength and discipline. You must avoid anything that puts your freedom at risk: with the law, on the job, and in the community. Take life one day at a time as you focus on building your foundation.

Remember, no matter how hard times get, there is no justification for making them worse! Even if times get so hard you think you're going to lose your mind, never give up your hope, dignity, or pride. If you stay patient and determined, you will overcome the hard times and find success.

Catching up is impossible. The past is dead, and what you have is the present, so enjoy it and savor every moment of your freedom. Too many get out and try to play "catch up," to make up for all the years they lost. Instead, build the foundation for your new life; start where you are now and go from there. You may feel that you've missed out on an entire period of your life, but it's impossible to go back and relive it now. If you try to reach for too much, too fast, it will disrupt the things you can realistically achieve. Don't dwell on the past and the things you've missed. Instead, dedicate yourself to making the rest of your life as fulfilling as possible.

Surviving Parole

The system wants to keep you on a leash for as long as possible. As a result, prisoners get out under some form of supervision, usually parole. In this case, like it or not, you are still doing time. You have to adapt to the fact that someone will be watching you, showing up at your house, asking you questions, requiring you to report and take drug tests, holding you accountable for what you do and how you do it.

With all the demands you face after release, it is easy to miss, ignore, bend, or break your supervision requirements, which often seem in conflict with your efforts to rebuild your life. Beware: half of the people arriving in prison each year are there because their parole has been revoked. Make sure you report when required, and keep your supervisor informed of your current address and job changes.

No one likes the nit-picking nature of parole supervision, but remember that it's an improvement over daily life in a loud, dirty cell block. Be careful: the longer you're out, the more you tend to forget just how bad it was. So stay alert and remember to keep yourself humble.

Money Management

Money is neither a god to be worshipped nor a magical remedy for our problems. It is just one of the tools we need to reach our goals. We live in a society that seems to worship money. Too many people define success as having enough wealth and toys. We often use money to measure our self-worth and our place in the world. It's as if we believe that money can solve all our problems and take all our pain away ... but it can't! Don't misunderstand, money is essential to survive in our society, but thinking it is all-powerful is a dangerous illusion. Money alone can never make life meaningful.

Remember: Your worth as a person can't be measured by how much money you have, nor by comparing your possessions with someone else's. Considering how hard you have to work for your money, make sure you hang on to it whenever you can. Continue to manage your money and develop a budget for your future needs. If you keep track of where your money is going, you may be able to find ways to cut your spending so you can increase your savings and security. Use your money management as a tool to help you achieve your long-range goals.

In the beginning, you will be hurting for cash and have to spend what little you have on basic survival. But once you are able to handle your essential needs, the time will come when you have an extra buck in your pocket. When you do, don't spend it; stash it! Build a nest egg, just a tiny bit at a time. Put it in a savings account where you won't be tempted to blow it. Consider everything you do and every penny you save as an investment in a more positive future.

Finding a Job

Employers need workers they can count on. If you show them that you really want to work and give them some basis for trusting you, you will find a job.

It's important that you begin putting your life back on track as soon as possible, and the most basic step in this process is to find employment.

As you pursue a job, keep the following in mind. First, you are broke and under great pressure to survive. Second, you have the system telling you to find a job and pay fees, fines, and living expenses. Third, you are anxious to reconstruct your life. And fourth, you want to rebuild your self-worth by becoming financially self-reliant.

As with any major effort, preparation is critical! Start by reviewing your strengths and weaknesses as an employee. Then develop a job search plan; this will help you organize your time and focus on efforts that have the best chance of success. Once you have a solid plan, keep at it; don't give up. Being consistent and persistent are major keys to success in job hunting. Finding a job is a job in itself.

Once you have a job, you need to hold on to it until you find a better opportunity. A key requirement for keeping a job is getting along with others. Be ready to accept instruction and criticism with a positive attitude, as a way for you to grow and improve. The faster you learn the requirements of your job, the more effective you can be as an employee, and the sooner you will be granted more recognition, responsibility, and higher pay.

For many newly released inmates, self-employment is a long-held dream. Self-employment is typically out of the reach of most released inmates until they have spent three to five years building a solid foundation. Running your own business is probably the hardest way to get started after release, not the easiest. You will need money to cover start-up costs and monthly expenses until some cash starts coming in.

Don't let this advice discourage you, only caution you: Working for yourself can be very rewarding, both personally and financially. But it will take planning and persistence. Spend your first three years in the community building the resources you will need - skills, money, tools, and relationships. Get up-to-date on new techniques and ways of doing business. Ask for advice. Develop a business plan and ask knowledgeable people to review it. But if being self-employed is your dream, be ready to put in the work it will take to be successful.

Staying Out

Positive growth comes in many shapes and sizes, all valuable because they bring you a richer, more fulfilling life. What matters in the streets is what mattered to you in prison: your freedom, your family, your future. Your goal following release is not just to be out but to stay out. And the best way to achieve these goals is to remain arrest free for five full years. Why? Because if you can stay out of the system for five years, you have learned what it takes to stay out forever.

Whenever you find it hard to stay motivated and focused, remind yourself of what truly matters. While the system may think that you are best controlled by the threat of being sent back to prison, your true motivation comes from the chance to achieve a more rewarding future. Thus, when things get crazy, stop and think about the importance of personal freedom, of being with people you value, and having the chance to actively pursue your hopes and dreams. Then get back on track and move forward.

One of the best and most practical ways to achieve your dreams of a quality future is to expand your mind and skills. This has two major advantages: First, it is great for your motivation, bringing fresh energy, hope, and achievement. Second, your ability to get along in the world, to be productive and improve the quality of your life, always increases as your mind and abilities expand.

So, once you have time and attention to spare from your survival needs, start looking for opportunities to learn and grow. As you get adjusted and have more free time, look around for a source of training that can lead to a new job, a better income, and a way to carry out your long-range plans. All it takes to enroll in a community college is a G.E.D. and a few bucks, and there you will find lots of good ideas and new people, as well as useful job skills.

CHAPTER 21

Pre-Release, Release, And Parole

If you are like most convicts, you've spent many years in prison thinking about what freedom will be like when you get out. Unfortunately, without preparing for life outside of prison, even the most optimistic can stumble, and end up back in prison.

Why do so many not succeed when they get out? You can bet it's not because they want to fail. A big part of why people end up back in prison is because nobody fully informed them of the many struggles that await them once released. And they also don't realize how life on the inside has changed them.

So here's some advice: don't expect that things are going to be easy once you get out, at least not at first, because, truth be told, it's going to be hard. You will definitely be tempted to return to your old ways – drinking, doing drugs, committing crime - time and time again.

The good news is that by reading this book, you're putting yourself in the best position to beat the odds. That's because you're getting facts about what can be expected on the outside, and you're getting practical advice for succeeding in situations where most fail. You're getting a plan for a successful reentry into society.

Of course, even if we provide you with all the information and advice in the world, it won't make a difference if you don't make the tough decisions to stay sober, stay disciplined, stay away from trouble, and STAY OUT! Everyone deserves another chance, and this chapter intends to help you make the most of it.

Preparing for Release

We often hear stories about the difficulties of readjusting to life outside of prison. It's hard to find a job, find and pay for a place to live, or get along with your parole officer (PO). A lot of people that were able to stay clean and sober in prison end up using drugs and alcohol almost as soon as they hit the streets.

Ideally, you should start preparing for release from prison the day you enter a correctional institution. Use your time in prison wisely. You should look at your time as an opportunity to reflect upon your mistakes, rethink who you are, what you might become, and then begin as a new and better person. This should include taking advantage of and getting involved with any and all self-help groups or programs.

These days, most prisons offer educational, vocational, and drug treatment programs, as well as a variety of different groups. Volunteers or contract employees organize Alcoholics or Narcotics Anonymous meetings, Bible studies, or classes on anger management.

All prisoners fantasize about all the different things they will do when they get out – wild sex, sharp clothes, new cars, fancy restaurants, and everything else. But it's time for a reality check. The cards are stacked against you. If you don't stay on point, you will be violated and on your way back to prison.

This is why it's important to carefully construct a post-release plan that prepares you for the potential struggles   you are going to face. You need to remember than your life may not have been all that lovely before you got locked up. Now, as you prepare to get out older and wiser, you could be returning to the same struggles you left behind.

Becoming Institutionalized

Prisoners live in tightly controlled environments, far removed from what lies beyond the walls. This is a world with a very different social system than on the outside. Depending on how much time you've spent in prison, you may have little memory of what every day social life is like in the free world. You may be shy or withdrawn and unable to carry on normal conversations. The longer people are in prison, the more accustomed they become to the routine of prison life, and the more difficult it is to readjust to living a free life on the streets.

By doing a lot of time in prison, you can become "institutionalized" because your life is so structured and almost entirely out of your control. This can cause an altered perception of time and an inability to plan a stable future. Most people living outside of prison take their freedom for granted, a luxury denied to an institutionalized inmate, whose state of mind causes him to live day by day, without anticipating or planning future events.

As an inmate, you forget the obligations and responsibilities most people in the free world deal with daily. You do not pay for housing, food, or transportation; there's no car to fix, gas to buy, bills to pay, or income taxes to file.

Getting Out on Parole

We want you to know how to survive reentry, avoid parole revocation, not catch a new case, and stay out of prison. Your struggle will not be an easy one, as there are many obstacles to overcome. In some ways, the biggest fight may be with yourself. So do your best to stay in control and avoid self-destruction at all costs.

Parole officers (POs) usually handle the heavyweights, the convicted felons who went to prison and are returning home after a long stretch in the pen. When you get out, you will be ordered to report to the parole office; do it! If you don't show up, your parole will be revoked, a warrant will be issued, and you will be picked up by law enforcement and taken directly to the local jail.

When you do go to your first appointment with your parole officer, dress like you are on a job interview - but don't be surprised by how others dress and behave as they wait for their meetings; they may not know as much as you do.

You may be subject to drug and alcohol testing, so avoid these substances at all costs. In addition, do not carry anything that could be considered as a possible weapon or part of one, not even a bullet or casing. POs may order you to stand with your hands on the wall and your legs spread while they frisk you and go through your pockets. If they don't trust you or you are giving them lip, they may even conduct a strip search and thoroughly check everything you are wearing. By nature, POs are very suspicious.

Our best advice here is to leave everything possible in your car or at home. Only bring your identification when you enter the building. If you owe the Court any money, the POs can even take the cash they find in your wallet, purse, or pocket. If you were silly enough to bring in your cash and they make you pay, at the very least make sure you get a receipt.

No matter what happens, don't argue with your PO. If you get out of line, he may handcuff you, and next thing you know you're in a cell again. Most parolees are required to have their urine tested for alcohol or drugs. Typically, you are required to pee in a cup in front of an officer. This prevents you from slipping in your younger brother's clean urine that you collected from him earlier that day. They can test you anytime they want: when you visit the office, or when they make a home or work visit.

Dealing With Your PO

POs come in all different shapes and sizes and with different personalities. They could be great, okay, good, bad, or all bad. It's important to get an early read on your PO's personality and demeanor. This will make a big difference in how you treat him, and the kind of treatment you can expect in return.

The great ones are the social worker types who become POs because they really want to help people. They believe that parolees can succeed in life if given a fair chance.

The good ones have a huge caseload and not much time to help you, but at least they bear no ill will toward you. They may be by the book, but to their credit, they might bend the rules a bit, cut you some slack, and maybe even a break, if you need it. But it would be better not to need it.

The okay ones are usually incompetent. You will be able to identify an okay PO when you meet one. He will smile, shake your hand, and then give you the same lecture he gives everybody, Okay POs can work in your favor, since they won't go out of their way to violate you. Just show him the respect he so desperately wants. When you must meet with him, just give him the yes-sir, no-sir routine. Be sincere; it must be true respect.

The bad ones are police wannabes. They applied for police jobs, but for various reasons were not hired, so they took the next-best thing, in their eyes, and became POs. They see the world in terms of good people and bad people. Do not give him any excuse to stereotype you as a bad parolee.

An all bad PO enjoys abusing and bullying parolees. More than likely he is one of those police wannabes who wants to wear a uniform with a badge and carry a gun. Too bad for you, this guy has never understood that his job is primarily to help parolees make it in the community. Instead, he thinks he should "tail, nail, and jail" parolees. This is the PO that is out to get you.

Going Straight

When you get out, you are going to be on parole. While on parole, POs will have the right to – and frequently will – search your residence. They can show up at your place of work or residence and ask all sorts of questions, including asking your employer and family questions about your behavior, associates, and whereabouts. POs are suspicious, and they tend to think that all parolees are up to no good and will eventually go back to their old ways. There are, unfortunately, parolees who have no intention of giving up the fast life, and they make the rest of you look bad. The bottom line is that you need to go straight, because you now have a criminal record. The cops have your photo, fingerprints, address, previous criminal history, and even your DNA.

You're now one of the "usual suspects," easily tracked or placed under surveillance. You are subject to having your parole violated if you're even suspected of committing a crime. It's time you just give up that criminal lifestyle, and adjust to a more modest, even boring, legit lifestyle. Most criminals do change over time. They just simply mature out of crime, and get too old or too tired of spending years locked up. On the other hand, there are a lot of youngsters out there just beginning the sad journey down a long road of crime and prison. They are usually the ones who are out to make a name for themselves.

Follow the Rules of Parole

When you meet with your PO, you will want to look presentable and avoid looking flashy. If you're all tatted up, wear a long-sleeve shirt. And whatever you do, do not drink alcohol or use drugs before you report to the parole office; it's best if you just avoid them altogether. If you want to move, you can ask to transfer your parole supervision to a different jurisdiction, but it can be a long process. You usually need to have a good reason, and the parole authority in the new area has to accept your case.

While on parole, your travel will be restricted to one county, a number of adjoining counties, or the state. You may need written permission in the form of a letter from your parole officer to travel outside the jurisdiction. When you do travel outside the jurisdiction, make sure you have the letter with you at all times; this will only benefit you, because if for any reason you get pulled over or stopped by the police, you will need to show them the letter to avoid getting arrested. When they run your plate or name through their computer, they may realize you are on parole in another county or state; without the letter, they may think you are on the run. It's best, and sometimes required, that if policeman talks to you, that you immediately inform him you are on parole. Subsequently, you will be required to report all police contact to your PO. The bottom line is, you need to know and understand the rules of your parole.

If you have any questions, don't hesitate to ask your PO. Otherwise you could make a mistake and end up in cuffs.

CHAPTER 22

Paroling To a Halfway House; Education

Most people getting out of prison are given an assignment to live for one to six months in a community facility, variously called residential treatment centers, work release centers, substance abuse treatment centers, and so on; we will simply refer to these as halfway houses. Halfway houses are facilities operated by government or nonprofit agencies, sometimes churches, where recently released prisoners will live for a few months. You may be so assigned; if not, there are good reasons to include such a reentry facility in your plans. Halfway houses are designed to help you make the transition from being locked up to living in the free world.

When you get short to the house, you'll likely be discussing your release plans or parole plans with your counselor. He or she may offer a halfway house and suggest how long you should stay there. You can either accept or reject the offer, unless it's already been written into your parole conditions.

You could even request a specific facility; it never hurts to ask, though there aren't any guarantees. It could be in your best interest to consider moving to a different city, county, or state than where you would normally parole. A change of scenery is smart; it puts you at a distance from old temptations that could lead you back into a life of crime.

Low-Income Neighborhood Halfway Houses

If you do get to a halfway house, don't expect it to be in a nice part of town. If you are lucky, you will be assigned to one that is close to an industrial or commercial section of the city. At least there you will be close by businesses that might be willing to hire you. Maybe you could even walk to work instead of having to use public transportation.

Most halfway houses are located in low-income neighborhoods, with high unemployment and crime rates. These urban ghettos are home to halfway houses, by whatever name, and parole offices are sometimes located there as well.

Considering they're living in the ghetto, it's not unusual for a parolee to walk outside his or her "residence" and be confronted by drug dealers, prostitutes, and gang members. This may be nothing new to you, so you can use your street smarts to stay out of the way and protect yourself. Just don't get involved with that way of life; the last thing you want to do is invite the attention of the police or halfway house staff. So it's best to keep your distance if possible, and go on about your business without getting mixed up with the wrong crowd, or any drama.

The street thugs know that parolees are living in halfway houses and are often looking for drugs and sex. So they are for sure going to be looking for new clientele and watching who comes and goes from the halfway houses.

Do everything you possibly can to stay out of the fast lane, or you will find yourself right back in prison. Your number one priority is yourself, and to not be arrested or violated. So, be smart and careful where you go, who you deal with, and where your curiosity takes you.

Earning More Freedom

First things first: If you are assigned to a halfway house, you usually have only 12 to 48 hours to report to the   facility after you step out of the prison gates. So start off on the right foot and avoid stopping at the bar or your
homeboy's house. The halfway house could drug test you and subject you to a breathalyzer as soon as you arrive.

Your parole conditions will require you to obey the rules of the halfway house, and those rules will, at least at first, put limits on when you can leave the facility you won't be able to come and go as you might wish. Most halfway houses operate a system where you can earn more privileges and time outside the facility. The name of this system might vary from one facility to another, but they generally follow this sequence:

1) Arrival at the halfway house. Make sure you are on time, sober, and drug-free.

2) Orientation, which may last several weeks. The halfway house will need time to receive and go over your files. During this time you can expect to attend meetings, or even classes, that the halfway house uses to help you become able to "fit into society, and so on, for example, classes about what to expect at a job interview.

3) Initial releases will usually be limited to looking for a job, and going to your work each day, or to arranging for and attending school.

4) Once you find employment and show that you can keep your job, or are attending classes at a college or university, or perhaps vocational training, you may qualify for evenings out with your family; eventually, you may be allowed to spend a night at home with your family.

5) Weekends at home. You may get permission to stay a weekend at home with your family.

In general, how fast you progress depends on many factors, including your convictions, the reports in your correctional file, your progress in finding and keeping a job, your payment of court-ordered and expected halfway house fees, how well you get along with staff, and the length of time you have left at the facility.

Living Arrangements After a Halfway House

While at the halfway house, you should explore possible living arrangements for when your time at the facility is up. You will have to find a place to live that is acceptable to your parole officer. Your goal is to save enough money while at the halfway house to pay a first month's rent and security deposit for a cheap apartment.

A temporary solution could be staying with a family member. You definitely don't want to move in with your fast lane homies who party all night and sell drugs on the side. You need a stable situation where you will not be tempted to go back to your old ways. If you are living with family or a friend, show some initiative and buy some groceries from time to time. If you have no money, then at the very least clean up after yourself, and offer to mow the lawn or do some other housework to compensate your stay.

Your best bet would be to find a small apartment or rental house in an okay neighborhood with low crime. Try to blend in and not draw attention to yourself. If the rental application asks the felony question, be honest. Whatever housing arrangement you make, be sure it meets the approval of your PO. After spending years in a prison cell, any apartment will look good to you. Try not to make the mistake of renting an apartment where your neighbors are drug dealers. After you find a place to rent, you will need to arrange for utilities, such as electricity, water, and a phone line.

Getting a College Education

Prison is an ideal place to begin preparing for college, even to take some college courses. Inmates have a lot of time to read and study, their room and board is free, and there may be few distractions. Prisoners who begin taking college courses in prison on their own initiative are essentially reinventing themselves and planning for a bright, new future.

Parolees often make great college students, but face numerous obstacles when applying to institutions of higher education, including gaining admission, receiving financial aid, and deciding on majors and careers. Regardless, you can go to college and get a degree. By reading serious self-help and educational books while still in prison, you are preparing for higher education. Perhaps you can even complete one or two college-level courses while in prison, or with dedication complete an Associate's degree. All this is usually done through the mail, or is in some cases sponsored by the prison itself. Reading self-help and non-fiction books, or taking correspondence courses, will help you start thinking about going to college when you're free.

If you haven't taken any college courses in the past, don't worry. In terms of academic preparation, all you need to be ready for college is a G.E.D. or H.S.E.D. You will have to figure out what will work for you in terms of your family obligations, social commitments, location, and what it is you are looking for in a school. You'll need to consider your options carefully, and then make the choice that fits you and your situation.

Remember that attending college and getting a degree is a commitment. It will take at least a couple of years for an Associate's degree, especially if you are taking less than a "full load"; don't get discouraged, just start and then stick with it.

Deciding on a College

One of the first decisions you'll need to make is whether to attend a technical school, a local community college, or a large university. Most technical and community colleges are less expensive and offer a wide variety of part-time programs. Some tech schools offer high school courses, vocational programs, and certificate completion programs, which may help you with your employment options. Community colleges may offer the same, but also offer more academic courses that lead to the Associate's degree. The Associate's degree would be the first step in transferring to a university and working toward a Bachelor's degree.

Be careful about unaccredited schools, colleges, and universities; check for reputation, and avoid schools that operate primarily for profit from government sponsored loans that they arrange but you have to pay off. Although it may be easy to enroll in these "institutions of higher learning," prospective employers might question their authenticity. You don't want to get a Mickey-Mouse degree from some institution that nobody respects; it could actually prevent you from getting some jobs. As a taxpaying citizen you have a right to attend public colleges and universities, just like everybody else. Provided you meet the academic requirements and can pay the tuition, you should be admitted. Just keep your head up, be patient, pay your tuition, do the work, and get good grades. All the hard work will pay off.

Admissions and Financial Aid

When it comes to applications, every school is different. Regardless, most colleges require prospective students to pay an application fee of $20 to $50 and submit it along with their applications. However, many colleges will waive this fee for financially needy students. When you apply to college, ask for a financial waiver on the admission form.

Most people getting out of prison who have been admitted to a college or university qualify for a full package of student financial aid. This is because the amount of financial aid you receive is determined in large part by the previous year's income, as declared on a federal income tax return. Because you were in prison and probably had no income, and were not required to submit a tax return, you should qualify for the maximum financial aid available. This can include scholarships, fellowships, grants, and loans.

Making sense of your financial aid package can be one of the biggest headaches you'll have to deal with as you make your preparations for entering college.

To help you understand it all, here are some definitions:

• GRANTS have no repayment obligations.
• LOANS must be paid back, and can carry different terms, including interest and repayment schedules. Most are zero interest while you are in school, and then relatively low interest after graduation. The loans are usually repaid over a 10-year period, but you can ask to have the repayment period extended.
• WORK-STUDY is a federal program in which you are paid minimum wage or a bit higher to work part-time on campus, such as in the library, residence hall, or cafeteria.
• FAFSA stands for Free Application for Federal Student Aid. This is the federal application that all students must complete if they want to be considered for student aid. You can go online and download the applications. Pay close attention to the deadlines for submitting your application.

Deciding on a Major

We encourage you to meet with an academic advisor as soon as you arrive on campus. Be honest with the advisor about your felony status so that he or she can appropriately advise you in your selection of a major. Many   professional fields are closed to ex-convicts. If you are a convicted felon, you should not major in education, social work, nursing, medicine, or law, because you will probably never be allowed to get a license or enter the professions; a criminal record stands as a formidable barrier. Sure, you might be able to get a degree in one of those fields, but you won't be able to work in those fields after you graduate.

CHAPTER 23

On Parole: Things to Avoid, Things to Do

There are many reasons why a parolee can get violated; most of these are mentioned in Parts Two and Three of this book. In this chapter, we will revisit four of the most dangerous temptations – alcohol, illegal drugs, weapons, and violence. On the flip-side, we'll point out some useful activities you should consider; they'll improve your chances of staying out.

Alcohol Abuse

Alcohol abuse is the most serious social problem in this country. Jails everywhere are constantly being filled with drunks. They are arrested for driving while impaired, getting into drunken bar brawls, and engaging in violent family quarrels. A lot of people don't even realize they are alcoholics until they are arrested and sent to jail.

Many parolees think they kicked their habit in prison, only to get out and end up getting drunk again, very few realize that they have maintained their sobriety because their access to alcohol was limited. When they get out, it's all too easy for them to fall back into old habits. These individuals may have chronic problems with alcohol consumption. They may commit crimes just to get money to pay for alcohol. In fact, a lot of people convicted of crimes were drunk at the time they commit them.

Of course, driving under the influence can also lead to a stretch in prison. Our advice to parolees who are restricted from drinking or having alcohol is to have no alcohol in your home at any time. It does not matter who bought it or who consumes it; when the PO finds it, the blame will be all yours.

Illegal Drugs

We live in a society where people have been led to believe that illegal drugs are the root of every crime imaginable. Every day, the news features a story reinforcing the idea that people on drugs are robbing, stealing, and committing all types of other crimes. True or not, it affects you.

If you just got out of prison and are going to apply for jobs, you should expect to be piss-tested. If your presentence investigations, rap sheet, or prison file indicates you have used drugs in the past, you can expect to be tested at the parole office, probably starting with your first appointment. If you have used drugs and your Pa wants you to take a urine test, we suggest that you be honest; most POs are more worried about your ability to tell the truth than your ability to stay clean. They might even accept that you are dirty and give you another chance; but if you lie and then are proved a liar, there's little hope.

Returning to the streets to mess with illegal drugs is not a good idea. Besides, while you were doing them all those years in prison, your street smarts were probably all dumbed down. You may have lost your ability to judge your surroundings. If you get out and start selling drugs, or even hanging around those who do, you will only end up back in prison.

Weapons

As a convicted felon, you are not allowed to own or possess firearms or other weapons. You cannot own a pistol, rifle, or shotgun. You cannot even live in a house where other residents own guns. While you are on parole, your PO can enter your home without a warrant at any time, without any reason or appointment. He can come in the middle of the night, alone or with police. The PO does not want to be greeted by a parolee with a weapon.

If you are on parole, you should make sure there aren't any weapons at all on the premises. For good measure, if the residents in your house have any weapons, they should be stored at another location. Thousands of felons catch new criminal cases because they don't understand that they cannot own or even be around firearms. The fact that the gun is owned by another person will not protect you from arrest and conviction. Never allow yourself to sleep in a house or ride in a car where any weapon is kept, regardless of ownership.

Violence

Parole officers are experts at testing parolees for anger or violent reactions. They might try to push your buttons when you report to their office, or when they visit you at home. Their goal is to get you mad. The PO might order you to assume "the position," face the wall, or go prone on the floor, with your hands cuffed, while another agent searches every room in the house. All the while they will be watching your reaction, even your body language. That's the type of games they will play when testing you for anger.

It's their job to be suspicious, to pry, to provoke, and to ask questions about your personal life, behavior, and associations. They could easily disapprove of things like your appearance, friends, family, or even the way you respond to questions.

So be smart, and no matter what they do, never show anger or let them know you are angry. Remain calm, cool, and collected at all times: emphasis, at all times, even when your PO is not around, because you can be sent to jail or prison for one verified report of violence or threat of violence. If your girlfriend or ex-wife calls your PO or the police and says that you threatened her, you could end up right back in jail or prison. So no matter the situation, watch what you say and walk away before you lose your temper. This is a very important reason why you worked on these problems before you left prison.

Keep in mind that the police can arrest and hold you with less evidence than the average citizen. Also, the prosecutor can convince a jury to convict you again with little effort, and the judge can sentence you to more time than before based on your previous convictions. Once you have that one strike, the second is a whole lot easier to get, and the courts would love to wash you with the third, which in some states means life in prison.

Save and Budget Your Money

Regardless of race or ethnicity, most men and women getting out of prison need to be educated in financial planning. You've been warned – you have a chance to learn this in prison, before you get out. Legal income is "slow" money, as compared to the "fast money" of illegal occupations. Parolees need to learn how to budget their income and save money so that they don't return to the life of crime.

After a few years behind bars, odds are that most of whatever you'd accumulated before going to prison has evaporated into thin air. It was probably stolen, given away or appropriated by your family, or confiscated by the cops or attorneys. You get out of prison with the clothes on your back and a few dollars. You have to start all over from the bottom.

You need a place to live, a job to support yourself, and you need to rebuild your family as well as your social life.

Practice in prison – save some percent of whatever pittance they pay you; save some percent of whatever money your family sends you; treat your job as if it's the real thing. Learn in prison the financial discipline and the "work ethic" you'll depend on outside.

Open a Bank Account

Avoid being like most parolees who probably keep the little money they have with them at all times, or keep it stashed in their houses. Your money won't earn any interest stashed in your mattress. You need to open a bank account and start earning interest on your money. A bank or credit union can provide you with interest on deposits, and possibly also free checking and a debit card.

All financial planners suggest that you set aside some money each month in your savings account. Ideally, you should have at least enough money saved up to pay your bills for a few months; this provides you with a cushion, should you lose your job.

Once you have a bank account, you can have your paychecks direct-deposited into it. Having a bank account will also make it easier for you to keep monthly income reports for your PO. Your bank records provide you with a way to verify how you make and spend your money. Your neighborhood bank is probably the safest place to keep your money. For day-to-day convenience, you probably want a bank with many branches, ATM machines, and a drive-up window, if you have a car.

Court-Ordered Restitution

You will probably be required to pay fees and fines, and to make payments on court-ordered restitution. This restitution is usually part of your sentence, and may be much larger than the fees and fines.

There are differences between fees and fines, and restitution:
 • Fees and fines are owed directly to the Court to cover costs associated with the conviction.
 • Restitution is collected by the Court (through jail, prison, or parole officers) to be paid to a third party, usually the victim.

In most jurisdictions, a parolee can be sent back to jail for failure to pay fees or fines, but not for failure to pay restitution. The reason is that fees and fines, like traffic ticket fines, are owed to the Court. This means the judge can issue a warrant for your arrest and then police can pick you up.

In comparison, restitution is owed to a third party; it's a debt. The most the Court can do is garnish your wages and place liens on your car or home. If you have no job, car, or home, then there is little they can do, except make empty threats, to make you pay restitution. However, not paying anything on your restitution will not make your PO very happy, so you are better off making small, regular payments just to protect yourself from being violated for something else. On the other hand, accepting responsibility is a sign of rehabilitation; if you scrape to make regular payments, and always demonstrate a sincere desire to completely pay, your PO will notice, and may then be less likely to bust you for something else.

CHAPTER 24

Landing a Job

Finding employment has got to be one of your top priorities when you get out. Finding a job after incarceration is not only pivotal for reentry success, it can also be a requirement for parole or a halfway house. After doing a stretch and with a felony conviction, getting a decent job could seem impossible. But stay focused on finding one and don't give up.

Get Started, Look the Part

Many people just out of prison believed they had a job lined up for when they got out, only to realize that the job fell through. So, you would be smart to have a backup job or two to fall back on. Regardless of the struggles you face trying to find a job, you have to get one. There are going to be obstacles ahead of you on your journey, so be prepared to overcome them, get around them, or go under them.

If you're staying in a halfway house, they'll likely have a list of employers that hire felons. Don't expect anything special; these are your typical fast-food restaurants that are looking for cooks and cleaning staff; they are roofing contractors, landscape companies, and other construction jobs. In order to help you reach these places to apply or to work, some halfway houses will advance you small sums of cash, for transportation and food. The halfway house will deduct what you owe from your paycheck.

It's essential that you dress for success when you start going to interviews in search of a job. Fresh out, you may need some help from your family to buy some suitable clothing. Ask them to loan you some money or take you shopping; take their advice about what's appropriate. You might also want to visit the Salvation Army or Goodwill to ask for clothes. Many of these organizations are more than willing to assist those that just got out of prison. Ask to speak with a manager, and be honest about your situation. Let them know you just got out and need clothes to start looking for work. More than likely, they will let you pick out some things you'll need. Again, you might ask for opinions about what's appropriate. Your time in prison, or some internal vanity, might have you picking out some item that won't help in your interview.

Job Satisfaction

It is important to find satisfaction in your job, but sometimes you must temper your wishes with your needs. When you have to take a job that you are not excited about now, you can leverage the feelings of dissatisfaction to push yourself toward whatever it is that you need to do to find satisfaction.

These things may include: submitting applications for jobs that you really want, but which are not available now; trying to work in an organization that has a similar philosophy to your own, so you can move within the organization to a job that is more fulfilling; getting the education perhaps required for certain jobs you'd like, but you are not yet qualified; realizing that your "day job" is your key to the future you really want, perhaps starting your own business, but needing work until your idea provides enough income for you to thrive.

When searching for employment, remember to consider these questions: What is it you want to do? What type of business would you like to work in? Which positions would you do well? What kind of jobs might you enjoy doing? Keep your eyes on the prize! Even if you must work for a while in a job you don't care for, remember that you are building character, patience, tolerance, and REFERENCES.

Job Openings, Applications, and Resumes

Most people look for work in the newspaper and classified ads. If the ad looks promising, call for more information and find out if you can fill out an application. You might need to go to the place of employment and fill out the application there. Looking for work online is the most promising. If you don't have access to a computer, go to your local library and ask for help. Popular job websites are www.monster.com and www.careerbuilder.com. You can also look for work on state unemployment office websites.

If you are hired, your employer will need your official name for payroll, taxes, and Social Security. Also, they will need your address, which may be the halfway house, and a phone number where they can reach you or leave a message.

On applications, when you get to questions regarding past work history and educational experiences, make sure if you have prison vocational or education courses or certificates, you mention them here, especially if they are relevant to the job qualifications. Some employers know that prisoners may have acquired work skills while doing time. Former prisoners may have learned how to cook, bake, landscape, do carpentry, lay bricks, work on cars, or perform basic clerical duties.

Some jobs require you to submit a resume. The big advantage to a resume, especially for someone fresh out of prison, is that you may not have to mention your criminal record. This means you could possible submit your resume and have an interview without the employer knowing you're a felon. But if asked, don't lie, be honest. It may be easier to get an interview if you have a resume. In fact, we suggest you prepare one and make many copies so you can give one to each possible employer. This way you have a carefully composed and typed document containing all your important information when you visit businesses to complete their applications.

All resumes should include your contact information at the top. Then, put a paragraph about education, then a few about previous employment, and then a few sentences about job skills and qualifications. One page is a standard length for most resumes.

When you are on parole, you will need a W-2 form and a steady paycheck to show your PO. A W-2 means you cannot be self-employed, operate your own business, or just peddle old junk on Ebay. You need a W-2 form paycheck once every week, bi-monthly, or once a month that states your hours, gross pay, deductions for taxes, and net pay.

Employment Tips

We often have to work our way up to the job we want, either because it is not available when we go to find it, or we need more experience, education, preparation, or time to get ready. Although we will spend time working at jobs that are not our preference, we can enjoy the interim more when we stay focused on our goals. Start by asking yourself:

• What kind of job or career do I want?
• What am I willing to do, learn, or sacrifice to get that job or career?

Before venturing out into the world of work, you will have to obtain necessary documents. The most frequently requested documents are:

- Birth certificate
- Driver's license or basic identification
- Social Security card

Next, ask yourself the following questions:

- What occupations or industries in your area are in need of employees? What are your employment limitations due to your particular crime?
- What is the income you need in order to pay for housing, food, energy, phone, child support, restitution, transportation, etc.?
- Which strategies do you think would be most effective for "selling" your attributes?

In preparing to apply for a job, you may want to create the following worksheet:
- Inventory your work history in and out of prison
- List your training, skills, limitations, and health considerations
- Gather all the information you will need to fill out employment applications. (Some companies only accept online applications; it may be useful for you to look through one or more of them to get ideas and learn what to expect.) Do you need clothes for your interview or new job? Check out *Dress For Success*, a global program that may have a location near you! www.dressforsuccess.org.

Interview Tips

You won't always get an interview after submitting an application – but if you do, and you feel that this job is one you really want, consider these tips:

1) Keep your answers short yet full of information; you may give longer answers if asked to clarify. Remember, there have probably been many applicants before you, so try to set yourself apart. Fine-tune your answers and bring your authenticity and vitality to the interview.

2) Determine what your key strengths and assets are. Be sure to state them confidently a couple of times during the interview.

3) Prepare for a variety of interview questions. Consider the challenges you have overcome, the difficult interpersonal situations that you resolved with others, and several success stories.

4) Describe specific situations and accomplishments. Generalities fail to show the interviewer your strengths and assets and how they can benefit the company and the position that is available.

5) Put yourself on their team. Show how you fit in with the existing work environment and company culture. During the interview, align your language with the language of the team.

6) Observe your non-verbal communication. Are you saying what you mean to say? Practice in front of a mirror to see if your eyes and your gestures agree with your words.

7) Ask questions. Find out what you need to know to perform the job. The interviewer will see that you are taking interest in the company and work environment. That is an important quality in a team player.

8) Be sure to talk WITH the interviewer and not AT the interviewer. Interviews are stressful enough for both parties. Keep it human.

9) Research the company. Is it a right fit for you? Can you get behind the mission of the company? How much can you

know about the work and the work environment before the interview?

10) Apply for jobs that you are skilled for and that you can appreciate ... even if only as a stepping stone to your next job. If you truly want the job, you must be able to compete successfully with others who want the job. Authenticity shines through your words and your non-verbal communication.

Resume Guide

A good resume will open the door for an interview. But do you need a resume? Some employers prefer a resume and others require only an application form. It depends on the kind of job you're applying for.

Resume Required
Professional, technical, administrative, and managerial jobs.
Sales positions.
Secretarial, clerical, and other office jobs.

Resume Sometimes Required
Professional positions: baker, hotel clerk, electrician, drafter, welder.
Resume Not Required
Unskilled, quick turnover jobs: fast food server, laborers, machine loader, cannery worker.

Write a Resume That Generates Results
The resume is a tool with one specific purpose: to win an interview. If it doesn't, it isn't an effective resume. A resume is an advertisement - nothing more, nothing less. A great resume doesn't just tell them what you have done, but makes the same assertion that all good ads do: If you buy this

product, you will get these specific, direct benefits. It presents you in the best light. It convinces the employer that you have what it takes to be successful in this new position or career.

Other Reasons to Have a Resume
• To pass the employer's screening process (requisite educational level, number years' experience, etc.), to give basic facts which might favorably influence the employer.
• To establish yourself as a professional person with high standards and excellent skills, based on the fact that your resume is so well done.
• To use as a covering piece or addendum to another form of job application.
• To put in an employer's personnel files (which they may check later for other openings).

To help you clarify your direction, qualifications, and strengths, boost your confidence, or to start the process of committing to a job or career change.

It's a mistake to think of your resume as your work history, a personal statement, or some sort of self-expression. Sure, most of the content of any resume is focused on your job history, but write with the intention to create interest and to persuade the employer to call you. If you write with that goal, your final product will be very different than if you write it just to catalog your job history, or worse, to make it any kind of manifesto, or even a plea about how badly you need the job.

What Not to Put On a Resume
• The word "Resume" at the top of the resume.
• Rambling "objective" statements
• Salary information

- Full addresses of former employers or names of supervisors
- Reasons for leaving jobs
- References

CHAPTER 25

Job and Career Resources

Now that you've decided to devote each and every day to your job search, the real work begins. This chapter will provide you a variety of ways to look for and find a job. They are all effective to a certain degree. The key, however, is to not just choose one of these methods; ideally, you should use them all.

Ask For Leads

Talk to everyone you know, and tell them you are looking for a job and what kind of job you would like to do. Talk to relatives. Talk to friends. Talk to neighbors. Talk to people in the community. Maybe you're a regular customer somewhere you would like to work. Tell the owner what you're doing; they might not be hiring, but may know of someone who is.

The best way to get a job, especially in tough economic times when the competition is fierce, is through someone you know. Through your contacts, you will be able to tap into what is considered the hidden job market. The hidden job market is full of jobs that are not advertised in the newspaper or on Internet job boards.

Part-Time Work

You may want to look at part-time work, because part-time jobs are usually not as competitive as full-time positions. In the beginning, it might be necessary to piece together two or three part-time jobs to make enough money to survive. Hopefully, one of the companies you are working for part-time will like you enough that when a full-time position opens up, they will offer it to you.

It's a good idea to take an easier-to-get job (stepping-stone or launch-pad job) even if you believe that you are overqualified for the position. An object in motion tends to stay in motion. There are many success stories out there of people taking a couple of stepping-stone jobs and then going on to find excellent full-time work.

Temporary Employment Agencies

Another way to expand your network and polish up your skills is to work for a temporary employment agency. These agencies hire you and pay you, but they "rent" your services to other companies that need temporary help. Some short-term assignments from temporary-help agencies can turn into full-time job offers. Many employers like the temp-to-perm model, since they can check out potential employees' abilities before hiring them.

Temporary agencies place their workers (you) in all kinds of jobs, everything from factory assemblers and warehouse workers to administrative assistants and accountants. This can give you variety and experience, increasing your worth.

You apply to work at a temporary agency just as you would a regular job, by filling out an application form, either online or in person, and having an interview with a recruiter.

You can find temporary agencies by looking in the telephone yellow pages or searching www.whitepages.com

online. Some agencies are national, with locations in major cities across the country. Others just have one or two offices in a certain area.

These are temporary employment agencies worth checking out:
- Acrobat Outsourcing (www.acrobatoutsourcing.com)
- Barrett Business Systems (www.barrettbusiness.com)
- Command Center (www.commandonline.com)
- Labor Ready (www.laborready.com)
- Labor Systems (www.laborsystems.com)
- Labor Works (www.laborworks.com)
- Link Staffing (www.linkstaffing.com)
- ManPower (www.manpower.com)
- Nelson Staffing (www.nelsonstaffing.com)
- On The Move Staffing (www.onthemovestaffing.com)
- Stafftnark (www.staffmark.com)
- Wollborg/Michelson (www.wmjobs .com)
- Workers.com (www.workers.com)

Job Training and Placement Programs

If you have been incarcerated – or haven't worked – for a long time, a job-training or apprenticeship program may be the way to successfully reenter the workforce. Job-training programs are usually offered by nonprofit organizations or occasionally by churches.

Here are some that may benefit you:
Goodwill. The Goodwill academy is for those who don't have much work experience. It provides paid job training at the organization's 25 stores and three processing plants in the East Bay region, which includes Alameda, Contra Costa, and Solano Counties. You can find out more at

www.eastbaygoodwill.org or by calling 510-698-7200. For other locations, contact www.goodwill.org, or 800-goodwill.

Delancey Street. Delancey Street helps those who have hit rock-bottom – ex-felons, drug addicts, prostitutes, and alcoholics – get back on their feet. The organization operates a residential program, with facilities in San Francisco, Los Angeles, New Mexico, North Carolina, and New York. Delancey Street is open to all ex-offenders with three exceptions: those who have committed arson, those forced to register as sex offenders, and those on psychotropic drugs.

During the first weeks of the program, residents work doing building maintenance and serving meals. They then earn their way out of maintenance and into a vocational training program. These programs cover a wide range of skills and businesses, from accounting and automotive repair to construction work and catering. Graduates have gone on to start their own businesses and work at top-notch companies.

The process for being admitted into Delancey Street's program is straightforward and does not take long; it can begin before you leave prison. Those who go for an interview and are likely candidates are accepted on the spot.

You can find out more about Delancey Street at www.delanceystreetfoundation.org or by calling 415-512-5104. Dr. J. Alfred Smith, Sr. Training Academy (JASTA). This academy, run by Oakland's Allen Temple Baptist Church, runs six- to eight-week classes teaching students about the construction and culinary trades. In addition, it offers mentoring and help with preparation for the GED test; it has a career center where people can take computer classes. Staff members also give advice on getting into the Green Jobs program at Laney College. You can find out more about the academy at www.allen-temple.org, or call 510-544-8910.

Center for Employment Opportunities (CEO). This organization, with offices in Oakland and San Diego as well as New York and Tulsa, helps people coming out of prison enter the workforce by giving them life skills, education, short-term paid transitional employment, full-time job placement and post-placement services. You can learn more about the organization at www.ceoworks.org, or 510-251-2240.

Apprenticeship Programs

One way to learn a new trade and get paid while you're doing it is to join an apprenticeship program. These programs are for jobs that offer decent wages.

Apprenticeships provide both classroom and on-the-job training, and pay participants a portion of what they will earn in the future while they are training for a new career.

In order to participate, you must be 18 years old and able to perform the type of work the trade requires. You may also have to prove that you are a high school graduate or produce a GED certificate. Another requirement is being able to read, write, and speak English, along with proof that you are a United States citizen.

The length of the apprenticeship program depends on the trade. When you are finished, you will receive a certificate of completion issued by the California Division of Apprenticeship Standards (DAS). In addition to the certificate, you will be officially recognized as a journeyman or journey worker; both of these have meaning and will help you gain respect in the eyes of potential employers and local, state, and federal governments. Since apprenticeships are sponsored by unions, they will also prepare you to be a successful union member and give you access to union jobs.

These apprenticeships are a great way to prepare for a job, but they can also be very rigorous. The plumber's apprenticeship program, for example, requires a five-year commitment, during which apprentices must work 9,000 hours of on-the-job training and attend 1,080 hours of training classes. The carpenter's apprenticeship program requires a minimum of four years, with 4,800 work hours and the completion of 612 hours of instructional classes taken at a carpenters' training center.

For more information and to explore the apprenticeship options available in California, visit www.calapprenticeship.org. You can find apprenticeship programs in other parts of the U.S. by checking out the U.S. Department of Labor Office of Apprenticeship Sponsors at oa.doleta.gov. The Office's database includes apprenticeships for every state.

Employer Incentives to Hire Ex-Felons

One thing that you would definitely want to bring up at an interview is that the employer can benefit financially by hiring you because you're an ex-offender. Here's how they can benefit:

1) Work Opportunity Tax Credit (WOTC)
The WOTC is a federal U.S. Department of Labor program, which promotes the hiring of people from specific target groups that experience barriers to employment. One of these groups is ex-felons, who must be hired no later than one year after conviction or release from prison.

The WOTC can provide an employer up to $2,400 in tax deductions for each qualifying hire, and up to $9,000 for long-term-family-assistance recipient hires. Employers may claim a tax credit on an unlimited number of qualifying new hires! To find out more about the Work Opportunity Tax Credit visit the U.S. Department of Labor Employment and Training Administration website at www.doleta.gov/business/incentives/opptax/.

Applying for the WOTC can be extra work that some employers may not want to deal with. Large corporations have tax experts on staff who can do the work; smaller or mid-sized companies might want to consider hiring a company like WOTC Solutions, which can do the process for a fee. Find out more at www.wotcsolutions.com.

2) The Next Step

You can also get help from The Next Step, a Shawnee Mission Kansas-based business, which manages the COFFE (Cooperative of Felon Friendly Employers) database, a nationwide database of employers willing to hire ex-felons. The Next Step talks to employers about the financial advantages of hiring an ex-felon and also provides job seekers with leads to ex-offender-friendly companies. It's just one more type of support that you can take advantage of. Find out more at www.thenextstep99.com.

The best thing to do is to visit your local American Job Center and talk to a counselor who can give you advice about these programs and how to approach an employer to talk about them. The counselor will help guide you through the process.

3) Federal Bonding Program

You can tell the employer about the Federal Bonding Program operated by the U.S. Department of Labor. The program was created to provide employment bonds for such hard-to-employ people as ex-felons, substance abusers, and those dishonorably discharged from the military. It's the only program of its type and offers insurance to employers to cover acts such as theft, larceny, forgery, or embezzlement that an employee might commit. The insurance ranges from $5,000 to $25,000 for a six-month period and is provided at no cost to the employer or employee. Find out more at www.bonds4jobs.com.

Search Online

Another way to find out about careers is to use a search engine on the Internet and search for the name of the career you're interest in, plus "careers" – for example, "carpenter careers", "construction careers", or "retail careers".

You can also go to indeed.com and search using a skill you'd like to use in a job, for example, framing, driving, forklift operating, customer service, cooking, or whatever. Pick out one or two careers you think are interesting, then search Amazon for books on those careers. Try to find a book that includes people's stories on what it's like to work in that career. If you find one you want to explore further, check your local library's online catalog to see if it's available, so you don't have to buy it. Other sites you can search are:

1) My Skills My Future (www.myskillsmyfuture.org)

If you have had work experience and want to know other lobs you can do with the skills you've developed, go to this website, put the names of the jobs you have done, and it will tell you other jobs that require those same skills. You can compare careers, find training, and search for jobs.

2) O* Net (www.onetonline.org) O* Net, another Department of Labor resource, offers information about various jobs. This information includes the tasks you would perform in a particular job, the environment you would work in, the tools you would use, and the knowledge, skills, abilities, and education needed for that job.

3) Career Info Net (www.careerinfonet.com)

This site, yet another service of the U.S. Department of Labor's Career One Stop, supplies extensive information on occupations, industries, and state labor markets, and includes helpful videos about what some of the jobs are like, as well as lists of training opportunities and how to finance them.

Job Search Websites

There are quite a few job search websites, and each of them is slightly different than the others, so you have to get to know them to learn which ones will work for you:

• Craigslist.org. This community bulletin board is organized by city and includes everything from personal ads to items for sale. Checking out this site is a must for job hunters, since many employers only advertise on craigslist.

• Careerbuilder.com. although careerbuilder.com tends toward professionals, it does have listings for carpenters, mechanics, and maintenance jobs, among others.

• Monster.com. At one time, monster.com was the most popular job search website, but the cost of placing an ad there has caused many employers to look elsewhere. The site includes all levels of jobs and is still popular with some employers, so include it in the sites search.

• Indeed.com, simplyhired.com, & linkup.com. These three sites are what are called aggregators: they draw listings from other sites, including company websites. Indeed.com, simplyhired.com, and linkup.com have listings that other sites don't and should be a regular part of everyone's job search. They all work the same way and may have some of the same listings, but each one pulls job postings from different places, so it's worth it to check them all out. Each is keyword and ZIP Code searchable, and you can sign up for job alerts just as you can with other Internet job boards.

• Idealist.org. This organization operates a site where people and nonprofits around the world can exchange ideas, share resources, and find employees. Jobs are searchable by country, state, and city, and by keywords and areas of focus, which could be anything from disaster relief or health to farming or countless other possible interests. In addition to job listings, idealist.org includes internships and volunteer opportunities.

• Opportunityknocks.org. Opportunity Knocks is an organization dedicated to helping nonprofit organizations find employees, and to helping people find jobs in nonprofit organizations. Its database is searchable by location and job type. The site also has a jobseeker center, where people can post resumes, and a nonprofit resource center, full of articles and tips on how to find a job in that sector.

• Allretailjobs.com. This website includes hourly and management jobs ranging from cashiers and clerks to sales executives and transportation/logistics experts. Its listings cover just about all the big names in retail, including Walmart, Costco, Macy's, and Pep Boys.

• CAcareerzorie.org. Career exploration and planning system.

• Jailstojobs.org. Information and tools to help ex-offenders find employment. Includes a national directory of free to low cost tattoo removal services.

• Job-hunt.com. Info and links to 13,733 employers and job search resources.

• Jobhunterbible.com. The official online job search resource.

• Jobstar.org. Reliable local information on how to find job openings, community services, company backgrounds, and job search advice.

PART FIVE:

SOCIAL SECURITY AND OTHER BENEFITS

Many prisoners get out not knowing that there are benefits out there that can help them get on their feet by providing necessities like food, shelter, healthcare, cash for day-to-day expenses, and support in emergencies. Part Five focuses on what these benefits are, how they can help you, which ones you may qualify for, and how you can get them.

CHAPTER 26

Social Security Benefits

This chapter will give you an overview of the Social Security benefits available to you in reentry. Social Security is a federal benefits program that provides cash benefits to retired people, disabled people, and their dependents. Social Security is a "pay-as-you-go" program, meaning that workers pay Social Security taxes, and taxes are used to provide benefits to Social Security beneficiaries (retired people, disabled people, and their dependents).

Public Benefits

"Public benefits" are government programs that ensure people can get basic life necessities. There are many types of public benefits programs that help people get food, shelter, healthcare, cash for day-to-day expenses, and support in emergencies. To qualify for any public benefits program, you will have to meet certain requirements. Each benefits program works a little differently and has different rules and requirements. Depending on your situation, you may qualify for several kinds of public benefits, just one, or none. This chapter focuses on the various Social Security benefits, what the benefits programs offer, which ones you may qualify for, and how to get them.

Federal, State, and County Benefits

The federal (national) government is in charge of certain public benefits programs that operate across the country; the state and county governments are in charge of other programs that are specific to their own residents. For some benefits programs, such as Supplemental Security Income (SSI) and Social Security Disability Insurance (S SDI), the federal government sets all the rules about who can receive benefits and how they get issued, requiring agencies in every state and county to follow those rules when distributing those benefits.

It's important to know what government agency runs your public benefits – who sets the program rules and which agency you apply and report to.

Can My Criminal History Limit My Ability to Get These Benefits?

It depends. With some benefits programs, there are no rules or requirements related to criminal histories, so you can and should apply to these programs. You can even apply for them while you are still in prison. But there are rules that may limit or deny your access to benefits if you have
• a certain kind of criminal conviction (your commitment offense);
• a parole or probation violation;
• certain kinds of unpaid fines, fees, or debts; or
• an outstanding warrant.
Different programs will have different rules and requirements about these issues.

Can I Apply for These Benefits While I'm Incarcerated?

Yes! You can and you should! Depending on where you're incarcerated, there may be special staff or programs to help you apply for them. Often, you can't start receiving the benefits while you are still incarcerated - but by signing up before your release, you can ensure you'll have access to those benefits soon after you get out.

Once I'm Released Am I Entitled to These Benefits?

Parolees and other people released from prison may be eligible for federal, state, and local assistance programs, but they are not entitled to receive any special benefits just because of their recent release. A parolee should investigate the various programs to see whether he or she qualifies for any of them. A person who is interested in getting any type of public benefits might want to try sending a letter to the appropriate office before release from prison, and should seek advice from a community agency or legal services organization once released.

In addition, parole agents should be able to help parolees apply for benefits. At a minimum, an agent should be able to provide a parolee with the names and locations of local offices where the parolee can apply for benefits. The parole agent also should have lists of homeless shelters, food banks, job training facilities, and drug treatment centers in the local area.

Nobody is going to volunteer these benefits. As a matter of fact, a lot of the benefits programs don't want to be bothered by ex-cons trying to get benefits. They may feel that because you broke the law you've lost your rights to the benefits. This is not true. Be assertive and consistent. If you continue to be refused or denied these benefits, you have the right to appeal. Many parolees are denied at first, but then get benefits once they appeal. More on how to appeal in the next few chapters.

GET OUT, STAY OUT

CHAPTER 27

Retirement Benefits

Social Security retirement benefits are paid out of money collected from Social Security taxes on individual paychecks earned by working taxpayers. For each year you work and pay Social Security taxes to the government, you earn "credits" – up to four per year. Generally, you will need forty credits (ten years of working and paying Social Security taxes) to qualify for retirement benefits.

How To Check For Social Security Credits

If you're not sure how many Social Security credits you have, you can call the Social Security Administration (SSA) at 1-800-772-1213. Ask that a Form SSA-7004 be sent to you, and submit the form. If you have Internet access, you can also use the online retirement estimator on the SSA's website by visiting www.ssa.gov.

Am I Eligible And How Do I Apply?

To get Social Security benefits, you must:
   1) be at least 62 years old; and
   2) have earned 40 Social Security credits.

You can start getting retirement benefits as early as age 62, but depending on your situation, you may want to
wait so you get a higher monthly benefit. This age may be 65, 66, or 67, depending on what year you were born.

You can apply online, by phone, or in person:
• Online: Visit SSA's website (www.ssa.gov) and start a new application at https://secure/sss.gov/iclaimlrib.
• By phone: Call the SSA at 1-800-772-1213 (TTY: 1-800-325-9778). A representative will set an appointment for you to do your application by phone. This toll-free line is open Monday through Friday, 7AM to 7PM. For each time you call, record the date of your call and the name of the person who assists you.
• In person: First, call the SSA to find a local office near you; or, if you have Internet access, use the office locator at https://secure.ssa.gov/iconlmain.jsp. Then call the local office to make an appointment.

Can My Criminal History Limit My Ability to Get Retirement Benefits?

Possibly – but it might be just temporary. You can't get Social Security benefits for any month that you:
1) are confined in a correctional facility for a period of 30 or more days in a row due to a conviction;
2) are confined to an institution by court order because you've been found "guilty" but insane, "not guilty" due to insanity or mental illness, or "incompetent to stand trial";
3) have an outstanding arrest warrant because you're avoiding prosecution or confinement for a felony; or
4) have been determined by a judge to be violating a condition of parole.

Once you qualify for Social Security retirement benefits, you stay in the program as long as you're eligible.

Although your benefits get suspended (paused) during incarceration, they don't get terminated (permanently ended) due to your incarceration, no matter how long your incarceration lasts.

If you're currently being incarcerated for 30 or more days, and you were already getting retirement benefits when you were arrested, those benefits were paused on your 31st day of incarceration. But you can apply to restart them once you have documents showing your release date. If you weren't already getting retirement benefits when you were arrested, and being incarcerated is the only factor disqualifying you now, you can start a new Social Security application before your release.

Can I Apply for Retirement Benefits While Incarcerated?

Yes! You can't receive Social Security benefits while incarcerated – but if you haven't applied before, and you think you may qualify, you can start the application process as early as several months before your release date.

Some prisons and jails have prerelease agreements with local Social Security offices. As the prerelease staff if your facility has such an agreement. If your facility has a prerelease agreement:
•   Speak to the prerelease staff. They should be able to help you complete and submit your application before your release.
•   The prerelease staff should also notify the Social Security office about your release date.
•   Ideally, if a prerelease agreement is in place, staff should start working with you several months before your release,

and Social Security should then process your application promptly so that you benefits will start shortly after you get out.

If your facility doesn't offer prerelease assistance, or you have trouble working with correctional staff:

• Call Social Security at 1-800-772-1213 to have application materials mailed – to you and to get help with your application. Be prepared to give your Social Security number and release date. If the SSA's automated phone system doesn't accept your call, you should ask a non-incarcerated family member to call as an authorized representative (AR) on your behalf. You will have to fill out an SSA "Appointment of Authorized Representative" Form SSA-1696-U4.

• An SSA agent will set a post-release appointment for you at a local Social Security office, and will advise you to bring your official release documents and tell you what else you need to do.

What Happens To My Retirement Benefits While I'm Incarcerated?

If you are convicted and incarcerated for 30 or more days in a row, your Social Security benefits will get suspended on the 31st day. You can't get these benefits while incarcerated, but you'll stay enrolled in the program. This means if your spouse or children have been getting benefits based on you Social Security eligibility, they'll keep getting them while you're incarcerated (even if your benefits were suspended), so long as they're eligible. This also means that once you have official documents proving your release date, you can apply to restart your retirement benefits.

(Note that "conviction" is one of the conditions of suspension; if you are in jail as a "detainee" pending and during your trial, your retirement benefits may continue.)

If you know that you will be incarcerated for 30 or more days, you should report this fact to Social Security, so your benefits can be suspended in a timely way. If you get any Social Security checks for any months during which you're incarcerated, these will be treated as overpayments and you'll have to repay them later. The amounts might get deducted from your future Social Security benefits when you're later released from incarceration.

After Incarceration, How Do I Restart My Retirement Benefits?

Before release:
Once you know your release date, notify your correctional counselor (or another staff member at your facility) that you want to restart your Social Security benefits. It's best to start this process at least three months before your release date. Some facilitates have a prerelease agreement available to help you complete and submit the necessary paperwork in a timely way.

If your facility doesn't offer prerelease assistance or you have trouble working with staff:

Call 1-800-772-1213 (TTY: 1-800-325-0778) to notify Social Security that you were getting retirement benefits before you got incarcerated, and you want your benefits to restart as soon as possible after your release. The toll-free line is open Monday to Friday, 7 A.M. to 7 P.M. be prepared to provide your Social Security Number and release date.

You can also ask a friend, family member, or trusted advocate to communicate with Social Security about your benefits on your behalf. Remember that you have a right to appoint any individual – such as a friend, family   member, attorney, or social worker – to act as your representative in the application process. Use SSA Form SSA-1 696-UR to appoint your Authorized Representative.

After Release:

Call 1-800-772-1213 (TTY: 1-800-325-0778) to notify Social Security that you were released from prison and want to restart you retirement benefits. Be prepared to provide your Social Security number. A representative will set an appointment for you at a local Social Security office; you will be reminded to bring your official release documents, and advised as to what else you need to do.

IMPORTANT: You can't get back-payments of Social Security for the months you spent in prison or jail. In other words, you can never collect retirement checks you otherwise would have gotten if you weren't incarcerated. However, you should be able to collect back-payment of benefits dating back to the month following the month of your release. So, for example, if you were released on October 1, 2017, you became entitled to start receiving benefits again as of November 2017. With no delays in resumption of benefits, you would receive your first benefits payment in December, and there would be no unpaid benefits. On the other hand, suppose you had difficulties restarting your benefits and didn't receive a first benefits check until March 2018, covering only the month of April 2018. You should be able to receive the benefits for November and December of 2017, and for January and February of 2018, because those were never paid, but did become due.

MIKE ENEMIGO & SHANE BOWEN

CHAPTER 28

Social Security Disability Insurance (SSDI)

Like Social Security retirement benefits, Social Security Disability Insurance (SSDI) benefits are paid out of money collected from Social Security taxes on individual paychecks earned by working taxpayers. SSDI is for U.S. citizens and lawfully present non-citizens (Legal Permanent Residents, or LPR5) who have earned a certain amount of Social Security credits by working and paying Social Security taxes, but who can no longer work due to a disability.

Am I Eligible For SSDI?

To get SSDI benefits, you must:

1) Have a disability: A disability is a severe medical condition that prevents you from being able to work. Once you apply for SSDI, the Department of Social Services will collect medical records to decide if you have a disability. Mental problems equal 100% disability.

2) Have a recent and long enough work history to meet SSDI requirements. It is a rule of thumb that you must have worked for five of the last ten years before your incarceration, or within your lifetime. Under these terms, you qualify under your merit. If you have not worked a sufficient amount of

time, then you have the alternative of qualifying under either your mother's or father's Social Security number. It does not matter if they are alive or dead, and it has no effect on their benefits. You will need their Social Security numbers, full names, and dates of birth.

Can I Get SSDI While I'm Incarcerated?

No – you will not be paid Social Security disability benefits while still in prison.

These benefits can help you once you have been released from prison, but you can't get them when you:

1) Have been confined in a correctional facility for a period of 30+ days in a row due to a conviction;

2) In any month that you are confined to an institution by court order because you've been found "guilty" but insane, "not guilty" due to insanity or mental illness, or "incompetent to stand trial";

3) in any month that you have an open arrest warrant because you're avoiding prosecution or confinement for a felony; or

4) in any month that you are found to be violating a condition of probation or parole.

One you qualify for SSDI, you stay enrolled as long as you still have a qualifying disability. Although your benefits get suspended (paused) during incarceration, they won't get terminated due to your incarceration.

How Do I Apply For SSDI?

Write to the Regional Director of Social Security asking for an application. Tell them that you have just turned in your parole plans and what area you are paroling to. Have the application sent to an outside address in case you are transferred, released, etc. Fill out the application and send it back to the Regional Director. Almost everyone that has been in prison has an emotional problem, a basis for disability. YOU CAN QUALIFY. They may deny your first few applications; however, on the fourth application, you will not be turned down.

You can also apply online, by phone, or in person.

Online: Visit SSA's website (www.ssa.gov) and start a new application at https://secure.ssa.gov/iclaimldib.
By Phone: Call the SSA at 1-800-772-1213 (TTY: 1-800-325-0778). A representative will set up an appointment for you to do your application by phone.

In Person: First, call the SSA to find the office nearest you; or, if you have Internet access, use the office located at https://secure.ssa.gov/iconlmain.jsp. Then call to make an appointment.
   Tips:
•   Before you start, you may want to look over the SSA's disability application checklist to gather the information you need.
•   If you need help with the application, call the SSA or visit a local Social Security office. You have a right to assistance from Social Security representatives if you need help due to a disability.
•   If you need benefits right away due to a financial emergency, ask if you can get "expedited" benefits.
•   You have a right to appoint any individual – such as a friend, family member, attorney, social worker, or other trusted advocate - to act as your representative in the application process. To do so, use the "Appointment of Representative" Form SSA-1698-UR.

Can I apply for SSDI While Incarcerated?

Yes! You can't receive Social Security benefits while incarcerated, but if you haven't applied for SSDI before, and you think you may qualify, you can start the application process as early as several months before your release date. Keep in mind that review of an SSDI application can take three to five months.

Some prisons and jails have a prerelease agreement with local Social Security offices to-make this process easier.

You have two options depending on your situation:

1) If your facility has a prerelease agreement:

Speak to correctional staff. They may be able to help you complete and submit your SSDI application before your release.

Correctional staff should also notify the Social Security office about your release date.

If a prerelease agreement is in place, staff should start working with you several month before your release, and Social Security should then process your application promptly so that your benefits will start shortly after you get out.

2) If your facility doesn't offer prerelease assistance, or you have trouble working with correctional staff:

• Call Social Security at 1-800-772-1213 (TTY: 1-800-325-0778) to have application materials mailed to you, and to get help with them. Be prepared to give your Social Security number and release date.

• If Social Security's automated phone system doesn't accept your call, you should ask a non-incarcerated family member to call as an authorized representative (AR) on your behalf. You will have to fill out an SSA "Appointment of Authorized Representative" Form SSA-1696-U4.

An SSA representative will set a post-release appointment for you at a local Social Security office, ask you to bring your official release documents, and tell you what else you need to do.

Note: If you become disabled while incarcerated, you can't start getting benefits until 1) you've been disabled for five full calendar months or 2) one full calendar month has passed after your release date – whichever is later.

I Believe My SSDI Was Wrongly Denied. How Do I Appeal?

Many people who apply for SSDI are denied at first, but then get benefits once they appeal. Considering the small odds of getting approved on the first try, be prepared to get denied and to go through the appeal process.

The following are steps you can take to appeal:

1) If Social Security decides to deny your SSDI application, it must mail you notice of this decision.
• You have a right to appeal. To do so, you must file a "Request for Reconsideration" within 60 days after the date you received the notice.
You can send it by mail, but it's best to file it in person at a local Social Security office. This way you get a copy with a time-and-date stamp, which proves that you appealed on time.
• You can also appeal online at https://secure.ssa.gov/apps6z/appeals/ap001.jsp.
• If you miss the 60-day deadline due to factors beyond your control, like illness or hospitalization, file a request for a "Good Cause Exception" to the deadline with your "Request for Reconsideration."

MIKE ENEMIGO & SHANE BOWEN

2) If Social Security then decides to deny your Request for Reconsideration, it must mail you a notice of this decision.

• Again, you have a right to appeal. To do so, you must file a "Request for an Administrative Law Judge Hearing" within 60 days after the date you got the notice.

If you can't afford a lawyer to help you with your appeal, you may be able to find free help by contacting a local legal aid office, a local bar association's referral service, or a local non-profit organization that helps with Social Security issues.

CHAPTER 29

Supplemental Security Income (SSI)

Supplemental Security Income (SSI) provides financial support for low-income people who are 65 years old or older and/or have a disability - regardless of work history. The federal government provides certain amounts of aid for people who qualify. SSI benefits are meant to cover basic necessities like food, clothing and shelter.

Am I Eligible For SSI?

To be able to get SSI, you must:
1) Be at least age 65, or blind, or disabled;
For SSI purposes, a disability is a severe medical condition that prevents you from being able to work. This is the same definition used for SSDI, and the same process is used to decide whether you have a qualifying disability.
2) Have very little or no income;
The income limit varies by where you live and may change from year to year.
3) Own limited resources;
The resource limit means that the value of things you own (besides your home and car) must be below a certain amount, which is set by law and differs for single and married people.

4) You must be living in the U.S. as a citizen or a lawfully present non-citizen (LPR); if you are ineligible for SSI due to residency status, but you are legally present, you may be eligible for the Cash Assistance Program for Immigrants (CAPI).

CAPI is a state-funded program that provides monthly cash benefits (similar to SSI) for aged, blind, and disabled non-citizens who are ineligible for SSI solely due to their immigrant status.

Can My Criminal History Limit My Ability to Get SSI?

Possibly, but this could be just temporary. You can't get SSI for any month that you:

1) Are confined in a correctional facility for that calendar month;

2) Have an outstanding arrest warrant because you're avoiding prosecution or confinement for a felony; or

3) Are found to be violating a condition of probation or parole.

Also, you can't apply for any Social Security benefits based on a disability that is related to a felony you committed. For example, if you fell while committing a felony and lost your ability to walk as a result, that disability won't qualify you for SS1. But you could still apply for SSI based on a disability that has no connection to your felony.

How Do I Apply For SSI?

You can apply by phone or in person; unfortunately, you cannot apply for SSI online.

By Phone: Call Social Security at 1-800-772-1213 (TTY: 1-800-325-0778). A representative will set an appointment for you to do your application by phone. This toll-free line is open Monday through Friday, 7 AM to 7 PM. Each time you call, record the date of your call and the name of the person who assists you. If you complete your application within 60 days of your first call to request information or materials, the SSA will treat that call as the date of your application.

In Person: First, call Social Security to find a local office near you; or, if you have Internet access, use the office locator at https://secure.ssa.gov/iconlmain.jsp. Then call the local office to make an appointment.

Can I Apply For SSI While Incarcerated?

Yes! You can't receive SSI benefits while incarcerated, but if you haven't applied for SSI before, and you think you may qualify, you can start the application process as early as 90 days before your release date. Keep in mind that review of an SSI application can take three to five months.

Some prisons and jails have a prerelease agreement with local Social Security Offices.

1) If your facility has a prerelease agreement, speak to correctional staff; they may be able to help you complete and submit your SSI application before your release.

Correctional staff should also notify the Social Security office about your release date.

Ideally, if a prerelease agreement is in place, staff should start working with you several months before your release, and the Social Security office should then process your application promptly so that your benefits will start shortly after you get out.

2) If your facility doesn't offer prerelease assistance, or you have trouble working with correctional staff, call Social Security at 1-800-772-1213 (TTY: 1-800-325-0778) to have application materials mailed to you and get help with them. Be prepared to give your release date.

If Social Security's automated phone system doesn't accept your call, you should ask a non-incarcerated family member to call as an authorized representative (AR) on your behalf. You will have to fill out an SSA Form SSA-1696-U4.

An SSA representative will set a post-release appointment for you at a local Social Security office, ask you to bring your official release documents, and tell you what else you need to do.

I Was Receiving SSI When I Entered Prison. What Happens To It While I'm Incarcerated?

It depends on how long your incarceration period lasts - specifically, how many full calendar months you spend in prison:

If your incarceration doesn't last a full calendar month, your SSI benefits generally continue without interruption. Once you've spent a full calendar month in prison or jail, your SSi benefits get suspended (put on pause).

• If your incarceration lasts for less than 12 calendar months in a row, your SSI benefits stay suspended, but you remain enrolled in SSI. This means once you're released, Social Security can promptly restart your SSI benefits if it has proof that you've been released and proof that you still qualify based on income and resources.

• If your incarceration lasts one year or more, and your SSI has been suspended for 12 calendar months in a row, your SSI gets terminated (officially ended). This means you're no longer enrolled in SSL If you want to get SSI after your release, you must file a brand new SSI application, including proof of your income and resources, and proof of your disability. Processing your new SSI application may take twelve to eighteen months.

I Believe My SSI Was Wrongly Denied. How Do I Appeal?

Most people who apply for SSI are denied at first, but then get approved once they appeal. You should be prepared to get denied and to go through the appeals process. Note: The rules and procedures for appealing SSI decisions are the same as for SSDI (described in Chapter 28).

CHAPTER 30

Other Valuable Benefits

As an ex-felon, you are entitled to the benefits described in this chapter. They are intended to help you reenter society after incarceration. We've provided you with eight valuable benefits available to help you on your journey:

Benefits 1-8

1) When you are released you may contact HUD (the federal Department of Housing and Urban Development) for low-cost housing, rent ranging from $29 to $125 monthly for two-bedroom apartments and houses. For more information write to: Department of Health and Human Services, Social Security Administration, P.O. Box 19001, Olympia, Washington 98507.

2) Upon your release, go to the Department of Social and Health Services for $180 in immediate food stamps, a housing voucher, and a clothing voucher under RCW 9.95.3 10. Once you have obtained this, then apply for the same thing from your parole officer. He can assist you in obtaining food stamps and has vouchers up to $250 for clothing for you once you are out. All you have to do is ask!

3) The Department of Vocational Rehabilitation will help you get started with your trade. Tell them the trade you work at and go to a store or a hardware store to price the clothing and equipment you will need. They will give you a voucher for up to $1,500. This is under RCW 72.02.100, which also covers receiving money for transportation when released, up to $100. This Department will sometimes pay full college tuition, including room and board.

4) There are two categories of people who qualify as disadvantaged minorities: ex-felons and Vietnam vets. As a minority, targeted job credits will give your employer a $3,000 tax write-off the first year you work, and a $1,500 tax break the second year, just for hiring you. If your employer trains you for some skill, the federal government will pay half your wages the first year, in addition to the tax cut.

5) The American Bankers Association, from their own foundation, will give you a $500 certificate. In the first year, the certificate must remain in the bank, though you can collect all the interest for the certificate and have it placed into your personal account. In the second year, you can go to the bank and collect the whole $500. The interest and the certificate are tax free. There are 13,000 bank members of the American Bankers Association (A.B.A.); you will have to write to the following address requesting information about the nearest office in your area. Write to: American Bankers Association, 1120 Connecticut Ave., Washington, D.C. 20039.

6) Minority business development and technical assistance: Depending on the type of assistance you need, you can receive a grant ranging from $10,000 and up. Applicant eligibility non-profit organization, objective: to provide free financial management and technical assistance to economically and socially disadvantaged individuals who need help in starting and/or operating a business. Contact: Chief, Grant Administration Division, Minority Business

Development Agency, Department of Commerce, Washington, C.D. 20230; phone number (202)377-3165.

7) The Small Business Administration will loan you up to $24,000 for any small business you wish. They will also loan you $500 for any vehicle you wish and $1000 more for any vehicle you will be using for work purposes.

8) Another address to contact for help in starting a business: Director, Office of Financing, Small Business Administration, 1441 "D" St., Washington D.C. 20230.

A LETTER FROM MIKE

I'd like to take this opportunity to thank you personally for reading our book. I hope you enjoyed it. The Team and I work really hard to make this happen from our prison cells, so your support is everything to us. Without you, there is no us. Straight up! You are giving us an opportunity to change our lives, and for that, we are forever grateful. We will continue to work hard in our effort to provide you the rawest content possible.

It would mean a lot to us if you could leave an honest review on Amazon. These reviews really start to add up and they help us out. Because we are in prison, getting the word out about our books is extremely challenging, so these reviews are especially important.

Please be sure to also follow us on IG @mikenemigo and FB/thecellblockofficial. This way we can always be in touch. If you can help spread the word about our books on your own socials, we'd greatly appreciate it.

Also, we invite you to visit our website, thecellblock.net. Here you can find all our books, our free online magazine, and profiles of prisoners looking for pen-pals, or who have books of their own you might want to know about. Lastly, please be sure to sign up to our email list so we can notify you when we have something new come out. Because I promise you, what you've seen thus far is nothing compared to what we have on the way.

Most Sincere,

Mike

THE CELL BLOCK

BOOK SUMMARIES

MIKE ENEMIGO is the new prison/street art sensation who has written and published several books. He is inspired by emotion; hope; pain; dreams and nightmares. He physically lives somewhere in a California prison cell where he works relentlessly creating his next piece. His mind and soul are elsewhere; seeing, studying, learning, and drawing inspiration to tear down suppressive walls and inspire the culture by pushing artistic boundaries.

THE CELL BLOCK is an independent multimedia company with the objective of accurately conveying the prison/street experience with the credibility and honesty that only one who has lived it can deliver, through literature and other arts, and to entertain and enlighten while doing so. Everything published by The Cell Block has been created by a prisoner, while in a prison cell.

THE BEST RESOURCE DIRECTORY FOR PRISONERS, $17.95 & $5.00 S/H: This book has over 1,450 resources for prisoners! Includes: Pen-Pal Companies! Non-Nude Photo Sellers! Free Books and Other Publications! Legal Assistance! Prisoner Advocates! Prisoner Assistants! Correspondence Education! Money-Making Opportunities! Resources for Prison Writers, Poets, Artists! And much, much more! Anything you can think of doing from your prison cell, this book contains the resources to do it!

236

A GUIDE TO RELAPSE PREVENTION FOR PRISONERS, $15.00 & $5.00 S/H: This book provides the information and guidance that can make a real difference in the preparation of a comprehensive relapse prevention plan. Discover how to meet the parole board's expectation using these proven and practical principles. Included is a blank template and sample relapse prevention plan to assist in your preparation.

THEE ENEMY OF THE STATE (SPECIAL EDITION), $9.99 & $4.00 S/H: Experience the inspirational journey of a kid who was introduced to the art of rapping in 1993, struggled between his dream of becoming a professional rapper and the reality of the streets, and was finally offered a recording deal in 1999, only to be arrested minutes later and eventually sentenced to life in prison for murder... However, despite his harsh reality, he dedicated himself to hip-hop once again, and with resilience and determination, he sets out to prove he may just be one of the dopest rhyme writers/spitters ever .... At this point, it becomes deeper than rap .... Welcome to a preview of the greatest story you never heard.

LOST ANGELS: $15.00 & $5.00: David Rodrigo was a child who belonged to no world; rejected for his mixed heritage by most of his family and raised by an outcast uncle in the mean streets of East L.A. Chance cast him into a far darker and more devious pit of intrigue that stretched from the barest gutters to the halls of power in the great city. Now, to survive the clash of lethal forces arrayed about him, and to protect those he loves, he has only two allies; his quick wits, and the flashing blade that earned young David the street name, Viper.

LOYALTY AND BETRAYAL DELUXE EDITION, $19.99 & $7.00 S/H: Chunky was an associate of and soldier for the notorious Mexican Mafia – La Eme. That is, of course, until he was betrayed by those, he was most loyal to. Then he vowed to become their worst enemy. And though they've attempted to kill him numerous times, he still to this day is running around making a mockery of their organization .... This is the story of how it all began.

MONEY IZ THE MOTIVE: SPECIAL 2-IN-1 EDITION, $19.99 & $7.00 S/H: Like most kids growing up in the hood, Kano has a dream of going from rags to riches. But when his plan to get fast money by robbing the local "mom and pop" shop goes wrong, he quickly finds himself sentenced to serious prison time. Follow Kano as he is schooled to the ways of the game by some of the most respected OGs whoever did it; then is set free and given the resources to put his schooling into action and build the ultimate hood empire...

DEVILS & DEMONS: PART 1, $15.00 & $5.00 S/H: When Talton leaves the West Coast to set up shop in Florida he meets the female version of himself: A drug dealing murderess with psychological issues. A whirlwind of sex, money and murder inevitably ensues and Talton finds himself on the run from the law with nowhere to turn to. When his team from home finds out he's in trouble, they get on a plane heading south...

DEVILS & DEMONS: PART 2, $15.00 & $5.00 S/H: The Game is bitter-sweet for Talton, aka Gangsta. The same West Coast Clique who came to his aid ended up putting bullets into the chest of the woman he had fallen in love with. After leaving his ride or die in a puddle of her own blood, Talton finds himself on a flight back to Oak Park, the neighborhood where it all started...

DEVILS & DEMONS: PART 3, $15.00 & $5.00 S/H: Talton is on the road to retribution for the murder of the love of his life. Dante and his crew of killers are on a path of no return. This urban classic is based on real-life West Coast underworld politics. See what happens when a group of YG's find themselves in the midst of real underworld demons...

DEVILS & DEMONS: PART 4, $15.00 & $5.00 S/H: After waking up from a coma, Alize has locked herself away from the rest of the world. When her sister Brittany and their friend finally take her on a girl's night out, she meets Luck – a drug dealing womanizer.

FREAKY TALES, $15.00 & $5.00 S/H: *Freaky Tales* is the first book in a brand-new erotic series. King Guru, author of the *Devils & Demons* books, has put together a collection of sexy short stories and memoirs. In true TCB fashion, all of the erotic tales included in this book have been loosely based on true accounts told to, or experienced by the author.

THE ART & POWER OF LETTER WRITING FOR PRISONERS: DELUXE EDITION $19.99 & $7.00 S/H: When locked inside a prison cell, being able to write well is the most powerful skill you can have! Learn how to increase your power by writing high-quality personal and formal letters! Includes letter templates, pen-pal website strategies, punctuation guide and more!

THE PRISON MANUAL: $24.99 & $7.00 S/H: *The Prison Manual* is your all-in-one book on how to not only survive the rough terrain of the American prison system, but use it to your advantage so you can THRIVE from it! How to Use Your Prison Time to YOUR Advantage; How to Write Letters that Will Give You Maximum Effectiveness; Workout and Physical Health Secrets that Will Keep You as FIT as Possible; The Psychological impact of incarceration and How to Maintain Your MAXIMUM Level of Mental Health; Prison Art Techniques; Fulfilling Food Recipes; Parole Preparation Strategies and much, MUCH more!

GET OUT, STAY OUT!, $16.95 & $5.00 S/H: This book should be in the hands of everyone in a prison cell. It reveals a challenging but clear course for overcoming the obstacles that stand between prisoners and their freedom. For those behind bars, one goal outshines all others: GETTING OUT! After being released, that goal then shifts to STAYING OUT! This book will help prisoners do both. It has been masterfully constructed into five parts that will help prisoners maximize focus while they strive to accomplish whichever goal is at hand.

MOB$TAR MONEY, $12.00 & $4.00 S/H: After Trey's mother is sent to prison for 75 years to life, he and his little brother are moved from their home in Sacramento, California, to his grandmother's house in Stockton, California where he is forced to find his way in life and become a man on his own in the city's grimy streets. One day, on his way home from the local corner store, Trey has a rough encounter with the neighborhood bully. Luckily, that's when Tyson, a member of the MOBTAR, a local "get money" gang comes to his aid. The two kids quickly become friends, and it doesn't take long before Trey is embraced into the notorious MOB$TAR money gang, which opens the door to an adventure full of sex, money, murder and mayhem that will change his life forever... You will never guess how this story ends!

BLOCK MONEY, $12.00 & $4.00 S/H: Beast, a young thug from the grimy streets of central Stockton, California lives The Block; breathes The Block; and has committed himself to bleed The Block for all it's worth until his very last breath. Then, one day, he meets Nadia; a stripper at the local club who piques his curiosity with her beauty, quick-witted intellect and rider qualities. The problem? She has a man – Esco – a local kingpin with money and power. It doesn't take long, however, before a devious plot is hatched to pull off a heist worth an indeterminable amount of money. Following the acts of treachery, deception and betrayal are twists and turns and a bloody war that will leave you speechless!

HOW TO HUSTLE AND WIN: SEX, MONEY, MURDER EDITION $15.00 & $5.00 S/H: *How To Hu$tle and Win: Sex,*

Money, Murder Edition is the grittiest, underground self-help manual for the 21st century street entrepreneur in print. Never has there been such a book written for today's gangsters, goons and go-getters. This self-help handbook is an absolute must-have for anyone who is actively connected to the streets.

RAW LAW: YOUR RIGHTS, & HOW TO SUE WHEN THEY ARE VIOLATED! $15.00 & $5.00 S/H: *Raw Law For Prisoners* is a clear and concise guide for prisoners and their advocates to understanding civil rights laws guaranteed to prisoners under the US Constitution, and how to successfully file a lawsuit when those rights have been violated! From initial complaint to trial, this book will take you through the entire process, step by step, in simple, easy-to-understand terms. Also included are several examples where prisoners have sued prison officials successfully, resulting in changes of unjust rules and regulations and recourse for rights violations, oftentimes resulting in rewards of thousands, even millions of dollars in damages! If you feel your rights have been violated, don't lash out at guards, which is usually ineffective and only makes matters worse. Instead, defend yourself successfully by using the legal system, and getting the power of the courts on your side!

HOW TO WRITE URBAN BOOKS FOR MONEY & FAME: $16.95 & $5.00 S/H: Inside this book you will learn the true story of how Mike Enemigo and King Guru have received money and fame from inside their prison cells by writing urban books; the secrets to writing hood classics so you, too, can be caked up and famous; proper punctuation using hood examples; and resources you can use to achieve your money motivated ambitions! If you're a prisoner who want to write urban novels for money and fame, this must-have manual will give you all the game!

PRETTY GIRLS LOVE BAD BOYS: AN INMATE'S GUIDE TO GETTING GIRLS: $15.00 & $5.00 S/H: Tired of the same, boring, cliché pen pal books that don't tell you what you really need to know? If so, this book is for you! Anything you need to know on the art of long and short distance seduction is included within these pages! Not only does it give you the science of attracting pen pals from websites, it also includes psychological profiles and instructions on how to seduce any woman you set your sights on! Includes interviews of women who have fallen in love with prisoners, bios for pen pal ads, pre-written love letters, romantic poems, love-song lyrics, jokes and much, much more! This book is the ultimate guide – a must-have for any prisoner who refuses to let prison walls affect their MAC'n.

THE LADIES WHO LOVE PRISONERS, $15.00 & $5.00 S/H: New Special Report reveals the secrets of real women who have fallen in love with prisoners, regardless of crime, sentence, or location. This info will give you a HUGE advantage in getting girls from prison.

THE MILLIONAIRE PRISONER: PART 1, $16.95 & $5.00 S/H

THE MILLIONAIRE PRISONER: PART 2, $16.95 & $5.00 S/H

THE MILLIONAIRE PRISONER: SPECIAL 2-IN-1 EDITION, $24.99 & $7.00 S/H: Why wait until you get out of prison to achieve your dreams? Here's a blueprint that you can use to become successful! *The Millionaire Prisoner* is your complete reference to overcoming any obstacle in prison. You won't be able to put it down! With this book you will discover the secrets to: Making money from your cell! Obtain FREE money for correspondence courses! Become an expert on any topic! Develop the habits of the rich! Network with celebrities! Set up your own website! Market your products, ideas and services! Successfully use prison pen pal websites! All of this and much, much more! This book has enabled thousands of prisoners to succeed and it will show you the way also!

THE MILLIONAIRE PRISONER 3: SUCCESS UNIVERSITY, $16.95 & $5 S/H: Why wait until you get out of prison to achieve your dreams? Here's a new-look blueprint that you can use to be successful! *The Millionaire Prisoner 3* contains advanced strategies to overcoming any obstacle in prison. You won't be able to put it down!

THE MILLIONAIRE PRISONER 4: PEN PAL MASTERY, $16.95 & $5 S/H: Tired of subpar results? Here's a master blueprint that you can use to get tons of pen pals! *TMP 4: Pen Pal Mastery* is your complete roadmap to finding your one true love. You won't be able to put it down! With this book you'll DISCOVER the SECRETS to: Get FREE pen pals & which sites are best to use; successful tactics female prisoners can win with; use astrology to find love, friendship & more, build a winning social media presence. All of this and much more!

GET OUT, GET RICH: HOW TO GET PAID LEGALLY WHEN YOU GET OUT OF PRISON!, $16.95 & $5.00 S/H: Many of you are incarcerated for a money-motivated crime. But w/ today's tech & opportunities, not only is the crime-for-money risk/reward ratio not strategically wise, it's not even necessary. You can earn much more money by partaking in any one of the easy, legal hustles explained in this book, regardless of your record. Help yourself earn an honest income so you can not only make a lot of money, but say good-bye to penitentiary chances and prison forever! (Note: Many things in this book can even he done from inside prison.) (ALSO PUBLISHED AS *HOOD MILLIONAIRE: HOW TO HUSTLE AND WIN LEGALLY!*)

THE CEO MANUAL: HOW TO START A BUSINESS WHEN YOU GET OUT OF PRISON, $16.95 & $5.00 S/H: $16.95 & $5 S/H: This new book will teach you the simplest way to start your own business when you get out of prison. Includes: Start-up Steps! The Secrets to Pulling Money from Investors! How to Manage People Effectively! How To Legally Protect Your Assets from "them"! Hundreds of resources to get you started, including a list of "loan friendly" banks! (ALSO PUBLISHED AS *CEO MANUAL: START A BUSINESS, BE A BOSS!*)

THE MONEY MANUAL: UNDERGROUND CASH SECRETS EXPOSED! 16.95 & $5.00 S/H: Becoming a millionaire is equal parts what you make, and what you don't spend – AKA save. All Millionaires and Billionaires have mastered the art of not only making money, but keeping the money they make (remember Donald Trump's tax maneuvers?), as well as establishing credit so that they are loaned money by banks and trusted with money from investors: AKA OPM – other people's money. And did you know there are millionaires and billionaires just waiting to GIVE money away? It's true! These are all very-little known secrets "they" don't want YOU to know about, but that I'm exposing in my new book!

HOOD MILLIONAIRE; HOW TO HUSTLE & WIN LEGALLY, $16.95 & $5.00 S/H: Hustlin' is a way of life in the hood. We all have money motivated ambitions, not only because we gotta eat, but because status is oftentimes determined by one's own salary. To achieve what we consider financial success, we often invest our efforts into illicit activities – we take penitentiary chances. This leads to a life in and out of prison, sometimes death – both of which are counterproductive to gettin' money. But there's a solution to this, and I have it...

CEO MANUAL: START A BUSINESS BE A BOSS, $16.95 & $5.00 S/H: After the success of the urban-entrepreneur classic *Hood Millionaire: How To Hustle & Win Legally!*, self-made millionaires Mike Enemigo and Sav Hustle team back up to bring you the latest edition of the Hood Millionaire series – *CEO*

Manual: Start A Business, Be A Boss! In this latest collection of game laying down the art of "hoodpreneurship", you will learn such things as: 5 Core Steps to Starting Your Own Business! 5 Common Launch Errors You Must Avoid! How To Write a Business Plan! How To Legally Protect Your Assets From "Them"! How To Make Your Business Fundable, Where to Get Money for Your Start-up Business, and even How to Start a Business With No Money! You will learn How to Drive Customers to Your Website, How to Maximize Marketing Dollars, Contract Secrets for the savvy boss, and much, much more! And as an added bonus, we have included over 200 Business Resources, from government agencies and small business development centers, to a secret list of small-business friendly banks that will help you get started!

PAID IN FULL: WELCOME TO DA GAME, $15.00 & $5.00 S/H. In 1983, the movie *Scarface* inspired many kids growing up in America's inner cities to turn their rags into riches by becoming cocaine kingpins. Harlem's Azie Faison was one of them. Faison would ultimately connect with Harlem's Rich Porter and Alpo Martinez, and the trio would go on to become certified street legends of the '80s and early '90s. Years later, Dame Dash and Roc-A-Fella Films would tell their story in the based-on-actual-events movie, *Paid in Full*.

But now, we are telling the story our way – The Cell Block way – where you will get a perspective of the story that the movie did not show, ultimately learning an outcome that you did not expect.

Book one of our series, *Paid in Full: Welcome to da Game*, will give you an inside look at a key player in this story, one that is not often talked about – Lulu, the Columbian cocaine kingpin with direct ties to Pablo Escobar, who plugged Azie in with an unlimited amount of top-tier cocaine at dirt-cheap prices that helped boost the trio to neighborhood superstars and certified kingpin status... until greed, betrayal, and murder destroyed everything....(ALSO PUBLISHED AS *CITY OF GODS*.)

OJ'S LIFE BEHIND BARS, $15.00 & $5 S/H: In 1994, Heisman Trophy winner and NFL superstar OJ Simpson was arrested for the brutal murder of his ex-wife Nicole Brown-Simpson and her friend Ron Goldman. In 1995, after the "trial of the century," he was acquitted of both murders, though most of the world believes he did it. In 2007 OJ was again arrested, but this time in Las Vegas, for armed robbery and kidnapping. On October 3, 2008 he was found guilty sentenced to 33 years and was sent to Lovelock Correctional Facility, in Lovelock, Nevada. There he met inmate-author Vernon Nelson. Vernon was granted a true, insider's perspective into the mind and life of one of the country's most notorious men; one that has never been provided...until now.

THE MOB, $16.99 & $5 S/H: PaperBoy is a Bay Area boss who has invested blood, sweat, and years into building The Mob – a network of Bay Area Street legends, block bleeders, and underground rappers who collaborate nationwide in the interest of pushing a multi-million-dollar criminal enterprise of sex, drugs, and murder.

Based on actual events, little has been known about PaperBoy, the mastermind behind The Mob, and intricate details of its operation, until now.

Follow this story to learn about some of the Bay Area underworld's most glamorous figures and famous events...

AOB, $15.00 & $5 S/H. Growing up in the Bay Area, Manny Fresh the Best had a front-row seat to some of the coldest players to ever do it. And you already know, A.O.B. is the name of the Game! So, When Manny Fresh slides through Stockton one day and sees Rosa, a stupid-bad Mexican chick with a whole lotta 'talent' behind her walking down the street tryna get some money, he knew immediately what he had to do: Put it In My Pocket!

AOB 2, $15.00 & $5 S/H.

AOB 3, $15.00 & $5 S/H.

PIMPOLOGY: THE 7 ISMS OF THE GAME, $15.00 & $5 S/H: It's been said that if you knew better, you'd do better. So, in the spirit of dropping jewels upon the rare few who truly want to know how to win, this collection of exclusive Game has been compiled. And though a lot of so-called players claim to know how the Pimp Game is supposed to go, none have revealed the real. . . Until now!

JAILHOUSE PUBLISHING FOR MONEY, POWER & FAME: $24.99 & $7 S/H: In 2010, after flirting with the idea for two years, Mike Enemigo started writing his first book. In 2014, he officially launched his publishing company, The Cell Block, with the release of five books. Of course, with no mentor(s), how-to guides, or any real resources, he was met with failure after failure as he tried to navigate the treacherous goal of publishing books from his prison cell. However, he was determined to make it. He was determined to figure it out and he refused to quit. In Mike's new book, *Jailhouse Publishing for Money, Power, and Fame*, he breaks down all his jailhouse publishing secrets and strategies, so you can do all he's done, but without the trials and tribulations he's had to go through...

KITTY KAT, ADULT ENTERTAINMENT RESOURCE BOOK, $24.99 & $7.00 S/H: This book is jam packed with hundreds of sexy non nude photos including photo spreads. The book contains the complete info on sexy photo sellers, hot magazines, page turning bookstore, sections on strip clubs, porn stars, alluring models, thought provoking stories and must-see movies.

PRISON LEGAL GUIDE, $24.99 & $7.00 S/H: The laws of the U.S. Judicial system are complex, complicated, and always growing and changing. Many prisoners spend days on end digging through its intricacies. Pile on top of the legal code the rules and regulations of a correctional facility, and you can see how high the deck is being stacked against you. Correct legal information is the key to your survival when you have run afoul of the system (or it is running afoul of you). Whether you are an accomplished jailhouse lawyer helping newbies learn the ropes, an old head fighting bare-knuckle for your rights in the courts, or a hustler just looking to beat the latest write-up – this book has something for you!

PRISON HEALTH HANDBOOK, $19.99 & $7.00 S/H: *The Prison Health Handbook* is your one-stop go-to source for information on how to maintain your best health while inside the American prison system. Filled with information, tips, and secrets from doctors, gurus, and other experts, this book will educate you on such things as proper workout and exercise regimens; yoga benefits for prisoners; how to meditate effectively; pain management tips; sensible dieting solutions; nutritional knowledge; an understanding of various cancers, diabetes, hepatitis, and other diseases all too common in prison; how to effectively deal with mental health issues such as stress, PTSD, anxiety, and depression; a list of things your doctors DON'T want YOU to know; and much, much more!

All books are available on thecellblock.net website.

You can also order by sending a money order or institutional check to:

The Cell Block; PO Box 1025; Rancho Cordova, CA 95741

Made in United States
Orlando, FL
22 September 2024

51798291R00143